Trafalgar

Battle and Era

Richard Stevens

ISBN 0-9550098-0-4

Typeset by Tradespools, Frome, Somerset
Printed by Antony Rowe Ltd, Bumpers Farm, Chippenham, Wiltshire

To Marcia, Madeleine and Harriet

ACKNOWLEDGEMENTS

I am delighted to express my thanks to those who have provided such assistance that, without them, this book would not have been published.

Cambridge University Library has allowed me use of their facilities for a number of years, which has been my primary source. I am most grateful to the assistance of many members of staff there over the years. I have also visited the library of the Royal Naval Museum at Portsmouth.

My wife, Marcia, and our twin daughters Madeleine and Harriet have provided much help, encouragement and support as the work developed. Marcia has typed the various editions of the manuscript. Madeleine has undertaken roles that would usually be the responsibility of a publisher.

Colin Walsh and Stephanie Zarach of Book Production Consultants plc have provided advice, and Captain Barrie Kent RN has answered some queries.

As publication approached, Samantha Cox and other members of staff at Antony Rowe Ltd and Ken Fricker and other members of staff at Tradespools have been responsible for printing, design and dealing with various ancillary queries. Their expertise has been greatly appreciated.

Lucy Waitt of the Picture Library of the National Maritime Museum, Greenwich; Andrew Helme, Curator of The Nelson Museum, Monmouth; Matthew Sheldon, Head of Research Collections at the Royal Naval Museum, Portsmouth; the artist Geoff Hunt RSMA and Cambridge University Library have all helped with arrangements for reproduction. I am grateful to them and their organisations for the requisite permission to reproduce the illustrations and the chart herein.

My thanks go to them all.

Richard Stevens

CONTENTS

LIST OF ILLUSTRATIONS

A HISTORICAL AND NAVAL INTRODUCTION

The French Revolution, which led to the outbreak of war in 1792, had a number of contributory causes. Weakness of the French economy was the underlying factor. Intransigence of the nobility and ruling classes when their assistance was sought precipitated a political crisis. The determination of the middle classes for change led initially to reform and later to revolution, and mob violence by Parisians provided impetus at critical stages. French participation in the American War of Independence had deepened the economic crisis and increased the desire for democratic reform.

The States-General met in 1789. In June, its third estate supported by other liberals forced a combined assembly and thus deprived the clergy and nobility of their majority. Radical fervour led to King Louis XVI becoming a constitutional monarch by the autumn, and reform continued in 1790. The royal family attempted to flee the country in 1791 but was caught and escorted back to Paris. Louis was reinstated as sovereign. The activities of the Jacobins, a radical political society that took its name from the former convent where they met, undermined the fragile constitution.

France declared war with Austria in April 1792. She became a virtual republic in August, when the king was suspended, the royal family was imprisoned in the Temple and universal male suffrage was adopted. Early military reverses were followed by victories from the autumn and Belgium was invaded. Decrees issued in November claimed to open the Scheldt to international shipping and expressed support to all people who wished to recover their liberty. The international crisis deepened and on 21st January 1793 Louis was guillotined. France declared war on Britain on 1st February, hoping thereby to unite the country and divert attention from internal problems.

Britain was in a healthy state on the outbreak of the Revolutionary Wars. Political stability was enhanced both by the expertise of William

Pitt the Younger, who had been Prime Minister since 1783, and by loyalty towards King George III. The economy was sound and had become strengthened by the Industrial Revolution; these factors sustained the war effort and enabled Britain to pay massive subsidies to her continental allies. One of the features of the world-wide wars fought during the next two decades was that various countries were allied at different times to both Britain and France.

Britain's navy was well prepared and soon established superiority at sea. Enemy colonies were captured, Toulon was occupied for a few months in 1793 at the request of French royalists and Corsica was captured in 1794. A French fleet at sea to protect a valuable grain convoy was defeated at the Battle of the Glorious First of June fought in 1794 some 400 miles west of Brittany. After some fighting on two previous days, the Channel Fleet under Admiral Earl Howe sailed from the south in line abreast and attacked the French sailing west in single line ahead; six French ships of the line were captured and one was sunk. However, Britain's army was not strong enough to achieve success and her allies fared poorly during land campaigns.

Three indecisive fleet actions fought in 1795, two in the western Mediterranean and the other in the Bay of Biscay, involved the capture of a total of six French ships and evinced hesitant British command. West Indian colonies were captured by British expeditions between 1794 and 1797. The Cape of Good Hope was captured from the Dutch in 1795 after engaging enemy ashore and an overland march. A particularly significant appointment was that of Admiral Sir John Jervis to command the Mediterranean Fleet: his tenure of command started in late 1795 and he introduced new standards of efficiency at sea.

A crisis developed in 1796 and 1797. The young French general Napoleon Bonaparte achieved success in northern Italy and various factors led the British fleet to evacuate the Mediterranean in late 1796. By now, Britain faced her three foremost naval adversaries of the last three centuries: the French, the Spanish and the Dutch. In December, a French attempt to invade Ireland was aborted off its coast due to inclement weather. The Spanish fleet was beaten by the Mediterranean Fleet under Jervis at the Battle of Cape St Vincent on 14th February 1797 off south-west Portugal as it sailed north to join in possible invasion plans and four Spanish ships of the line were captured.

Grievances on the part of seamen led to fleet mutinies in home waters and the temporary paralysis of many ships of the line. Amongst these was the fact that their pay had not risen since 1653. The affair at Spithead, the navy's anchorage off Portsmouth, was settled amicably whereas excesses at the Nore, off Sheerness, resulted in a number of mutineers being hanged. At one stage, Admiral Duncan had blockaded the Dutch fleet with only two ships and by signalling to an imaginary fleet over the horizon.

The Dutch fleet was beaten by Duncan's North Sea Fleet at the Battle of Camperdown off the Dutch coast on 11th October 1797. As the Dutch sailed along the coast, the British in two divisions engaged the Dutch from seaward before they reached shallow water and achieved an emphatic victory. The remnant of the Dutch fleet surrendered without fighting in 1799.

Austria made peace with France in October 1797, leaving Britain virtually alone in the fight against France.

Bonaparte conquered Egypt in 1798 but his fleet was defeated by Rear-Admiral Sir Horatio Nelson's ships at the Battle of the Nile. Having scoured the Mediterranean trying to find them, the French were brought to action on 1st August whilst anchored in Aboukir Bay. During a night action the British attacked the moored French line from both seaward and landward. The French flagship exploded, nine ships of the line surrendered and another was destroyed by her crew. This victory encouraged the creation of the Second Coalition of allies.

Insurrection in Ireland was crushed in 1798. A French squadron providing support was defeated off Ireland.

Naval activity in the Mediterranean continued. Minorca was captured for use as a base and the navy undertook operations on the Italian mainland. Two ships of the line inspired the Turkish defence of Acre in 1799, thereby halting the advance of Bonaparte's army towards Syria. A French fleet sent to the Mediterranean failed to engage the dispersed British squadrons. Malta surrendered after a lengthy siege in 1800. However, France generally had superiority on land and Austria made peace again with France in 1801.

The League of Armed Neutrality was revived in 1800 by Baltic countries hostile to Britain seeking to contest her claims to search neutral shipping for contraband of war. A fleet under Admiral Sir Hyde Parker was therefore despatched in 1801. On 2nd April Vice-Admiral Lord Nelson led part of it into action at the Battle of Copenhagen and overwhelmed the Danish line of miscellaneous vessels moored offshore defending the capital.

A British army was landed in Egypt in 1801 and drove the French out of the country. A Franco-Spanish squadron despatched in support was defeated in July in the Straits of Gibraltar.

The war had led to stalemate between British supremacy at sea and French superiority on land. Both countries realised the benefits of peace and, following negotiations started in 1801, the Treaty of Amiens was signed on 27th March 1802.

The period of uneasy peace following the treaty was dominated by the territorial ambitions of Bonaparte, now the first consul. Negotiations failed to resolve the crisis and France was presented with an ultimatum demanding not only French withdrawal from Holland and Switzerland but also British retention of Malta. France refused and on 18th May 1803 Britain declared war.

During the early years of the Napoleonic Wars, France aspired to invade England. It was not until 1805 that the invasion flotilla was deemed ready and the Emperor Napoleon (as Bonaparte now was) ordered fleet movements to cover his planned invasion. These were thwarted by the navy's activity during the year and on 21st October the Franco-Spanish fleet was decisively defeated and lost 18 ships of the line at the Battle of Trafalgar off Spain's Atlantic coast. These events are covered in Chapter 2. A French squadron, having escaped from Brest, was defeated off the island of Hispaniola in the West Indies in February 1806.

Sicilian vulnerability continued to cause concern and some operations were undertaken on the Italian mainland. In 1807, a squadron forced the Dardanelles but failed to take the Turkish fleet and an expedition to Copenhagen secured the surrender of the Danish fleet. Peripheral expeditions were undertaken in South America and elsewhere.

British naval supremacy was offset by Napoleon's military victories over Austria, Russia and Prussia from late 1805 to 1807.

Napoleon decided that the only way to defeat Britain was to institute an economic blockade, which became known as the Continental System. This scheme was launched by decrees issued in late 1806 and reinforced by more in 1807. Britain responded by issuing orders in council aimed against foreign trade. British trade declined during the second half of 1807 and early 1808. In 1808, Napoleon decided to enforce his rule on Spain, hitherto an ally, which responded by rising in revolt. Britain sent an army to help the Spaniards, and the navy evacuated Moore's army at Corunna in 1809. Meanwhile, British trade improved steadily.

The navy's role as the strongest component in the struggle against France remained and its resources continued to be stretched in many theatres around the world. More enemy colonies were captured from 1808 to 1812, thereby depriving France of her bases outside Europe. The Baltic Fleet, from 1808 to 1812, under Vice-Admiral Sir James Saumarez combined fighting and diplomacy. A French fleet was attacked with fire and explosion vessels whilst anchored in the Basque Roads near Rochefort in 1809. The navy's support of Wellington's army during the Peninsular War was of great significance, particularly because it enabled the army to remain much better supplied than were the French. Coastal forays mounted by the navy achieved successes, diverted French troops away from the main military conflicts and enabled supply lines to the advancing army to be shortened.

Napoleon's decision to invade Russia in 1812 meant that France was fighting on two fronts and she suffered huge losses during the Russian campaign. These were followed by military defeats in 1813 and 1814. France sought peace and Napoleon was taken to captivity on the island of Elba. Diplomats attending the Congress of Vienna began to shape a peace.

War between Britain and America had broken out in 1812 due to British search of American ships. Although Napoleon's scheming had led to the war, France and America fought separately. Britain experienced defeat in some early duels with stronger American ships and in two actions between flotillas of small vessels on the Great Lakes. However, British forces imposed an increasingly tight grip upon the war before peace was signed in 1814.

Napoleon's escape in 1815 led to the Campaign of the Hundred Days and his final defeat at the Battle of Waterloo. He fled to the Biscay coast, where he surrendered to the *Bellerophon*, a British ship of the line. He was taken to the remote island of St Helena in the South Atlantic, where he was held captive for the rest of his life. The Congress of Vienna concluded a lasting treaty that was to result in relative peace in Europe for a century.

The navy's main roles were to ensure maritime supremacy, prevent invasion, protect trade and mount offensive operations. The British navy, in contrast to that of France, spent much of its time at sea and thereby enhanced its maritime skills. Watching France's main ports, Brest on the Brittany coast and Toulon in the Mediterranean, was important and blockading the fleets therein reduced the risk of invasion. The convoy system proved to be an excellent means of reducing mercantile losses. Commerce enhanced national wealth, increased Britain's global importance and served as a nursery for seamen.

The six decisive fleet battles and other major actions fought during the era have been mentioned. Depending upon how one chooses to calculate, Britain captured or destroyed over 60 enemy ships of the line in these actions for the loss of only one ship.

Activities ashore included combined operations with the army as well as those mounted by the navy alone. Numerous enemy colonies and islands, many of them in the West and East Indies, were captured. Amongst these were Malta, the Cape of Good Hope and Ceylon (now Sri Lanka), all of which remained in British possession after the peace.

Many minor actions were fought at sea. Single ship duels were fought between frigates and smaller vessels. Privateers, which were private vessels to whose owners a belligerent government issued letters of marque entitling them to capture enemy vessels for profit, became a scourge upon British trade. Enemy merchantmen were attacked. Cutting-out actions, which involved capturing moored enemy vessels, were undertaken.

The Admiralty was responsible for warfare and operations. The Admiralty Board was composed of seven commissioners presided over by the First Lord, who had a seat in the cabinet. The six junior lords were admirals, captains or civilians; some had seats in Parliament. The Admiralty was located in Whitehall. Other boards, such as the Navy Board, had lesser responsibilities.

The six major dockyards were at Portsmouth, Plymouth, Chatham, Sheerness, Deptford and Woolwich. The waterfronts of the six major yards had wharves intersected by entrances to docks, building slips and channels. They built ships on building slips, which sloped down slightly towards the water for launching. Ships were repaired in dry docks after the dock had been drained. Some yards had a basin or wet dock, which was an enclosed area of water that could be kept at high tide level; ships could be inspected and repaired above the waterline and moved between the basin and docks leading off it irrespective of the tide. Mast ponds enabled timber for masts and yards to be held underwater to retain suppleness. Spinners produced yarns by walking along the spinning floor, and on the laying floor firstly yarns and then strands were twisted together to form ropes. Spinning and laying floors had to be extremely long; in some yards they were combined in a double ropehouse. In sail lofts, on the uppermost floor of some buildings with a large floor space, canvas was laid out and stitched to make sails. Other facilities included boathouses, workshops, store-houses, offices, timber seasoning sheds, saw pits, kilns and horse-powered cranes. The block mills at Portsmouth were built between 1802 and 1806 for making blocks and are said to be the world's first factory using machine tools for mass production.

Lesser yards, depots and bases existed at home and abroad. The majority of ships were built in private yards such as Buckler's Hard on the River Beaulieu in Hampshire. Other naval facilities ashore included hospitals and marine barracks. Signal stations on the British coast kept watch for invasion, enemy privateers and smugglers.

The rating system of ships was based upon the number of guns carried. Rated ships had a nominal armament of at least 20 guns and were commanded by a post captain whereas lesser vessels were under a commander or junior officer. Carronades, which were short-range guns, were introduced in such a manner that the actual number of guns carried frequently exceeded the nominal rating. A ship's name and rating were often cited together.

Ships of the line were thus termed because they formed the line of battle. A ship was usually regarded as such only if she carried at least 64 guns. First rate ships of at least 100 guns and second rate ships of 98 or 90 guns were three-deckers, with three complete gun decks running the length of the ship. Third rate ships were two-deckers, of which the largest were a few ships of 84 or 80 guns. The large majority of third rates mounted 74 guns and were often called seventy-fours. They were the most numerous ships of the line and thus formed the backbone of the fleets. The 32-pounder was the standard cannon on lower decks of ships rated 74 guns or more. The smallest type of third rate was the weaker sixty-four. Ships of the line were deployed mainly in fleets or squadrons.

The fourth rate comprised two-deckers from 60 to 50 guns. They were usually employed on stations where their lighter draught might be an asset or where a relatively minor naval presence was required.

Frigates served as fleet attendant, cruiser and convoy escort. Most of the few frigates of 44 or 40 guns mounted 24-pounders on their single gun deck. The 18-pounder frigate of 38 or 36 guns became firmly established during the Napoleonic Wars as the main type of frigate. The 32-gun 12-pounder frigate had been the most numerous category in 1793. A 28-gun frigate carried 9-pounders. Frigates were good sailing ships and carried sufficient provisions that they could operate independently for a lengthy period, and were popular ships to serve on.

Sixth rate ships reduced in number during the era. Those other than 28-gun frigates were known as post ships and mounted from 26 to 20 guns.

The navy had many unrated vessels. Sloops were ship-rigged with three masts or brig-rigged with square sails on two masts and were thus often referred to simply as ship-sloops or brig-sloops. Other vessels included cutters, luggers, and non-combatant vessels. Many unrated vessels were hired from private owners. Unrated vessels were typically flush-decked and steered by a tiller on the quarterdeck. Some passages in this chapter, which concentrates upon rated ships, apply only in modified form to these smaller vessels.

The head of the ship with the figurehead was a collection of features forward of the bows. Four large anchors were carried well forward on larger vessels. Channels were long, narrow platforms projecting from the ship's side abreast of each mast to spread the lower rigging. Rows of rectangular gun ports, each with a lid hinged at the top, ranged along the hull. They were often open to provide ventilation and light. Wooden steps for climbing were fitted near the aft end of the waist from the waterline up the ship's side; ropes might be suspended from above to assist climbing. The highest part of the stern was the taffrail. The stern was often decorated with ornate carving. Rated ships had stern windows across the stern, occasionally with a projecting stern-walk projecting beyond the stern, and enclosed quarter galleries on each side. Copper sheathing below the waterline protected the timbers from the ravages of the teredo or ship worm, which had a voracious appetite for wood, and improved the ship's sailing.

The hold was the lowest part of the interior of the hull and contained the bulk of the ship's provisions and stores. Bulkheads formed smaller areas such as the spirit room aft. Further forward was an area where provisions were stored in wooden casks resting on the ballast. The pump well was amidships, where bilge water would be deepest and from where it was pumped up to the lower deck by valves attached to an endless chain placed in a casing. Further forward on board ships of the line, powder was stored in the main magazine. Many vessels had other magazines or powder rooms elsewhere.

The orlop deck was the first deck above the hold and was below water level. Cables, spare sails and other equipment were stowed here. The cockpit provided accommodation for midshipmen and other officers.

The lower deck of a ship of the line was the main living area for the men. Inboard were various fittings. Hatchways were usually covered by gratings, which were sturdy frameworks of crossed wooden bars. Ladderways with ladders were nearby. Capstans were used to weigh anchor and lift heavy objects, with men pushing on bars inserted into holes in the drumhead on the deck above. Long winches enabled several men to man the pumps together. The deck had low headroom and was dimly lit, poorly ventilated and often crowded. Above was the main or upper deck, and three-deckers also had a middle deck. On the deck above the lower deck on board ships of the line, the galley with its stove was forward and senior officers messed in the wardroom astern. An admiral's quarters aboard a three-decker were on the upper deck aft.

The forecastle was the uppermost deck forward. Its features included the fore mast, the galley chimney with its cowl and the belfry with the ship's bell. Hammocks in nets here and running aft along the ship's sides gave some protection from enemy shot.

The waist was the area between the forecastle and quarterdeck. Inboard along each side was a gangway, also known as a gangboard, connecting forecastle and quarterdeck. The space inboard might be decked or open with booms or skid beams laid athwartships; boats and spare spars were stowed here.

The quarterdeck extended aft from near the main mast. It was here that the ship was commanded. The after part of a ship of the line's quarterdeck was enclosed by the poop deck above it. Just aft of the break of the poop were the binnacle and wheel on either side of which was a cabin with windows. Further aft were the captain's day, dining and sleeping cabins.

The poop was the highest deck aft on ships of the line. Just aft of the mizen mast was a skylight known as the companion. There was then a relatively spare area of deck reaching aft to the taffrail, where

---

(*overleaf*)

Diagram of a three-decked ship of the line in a fair wind

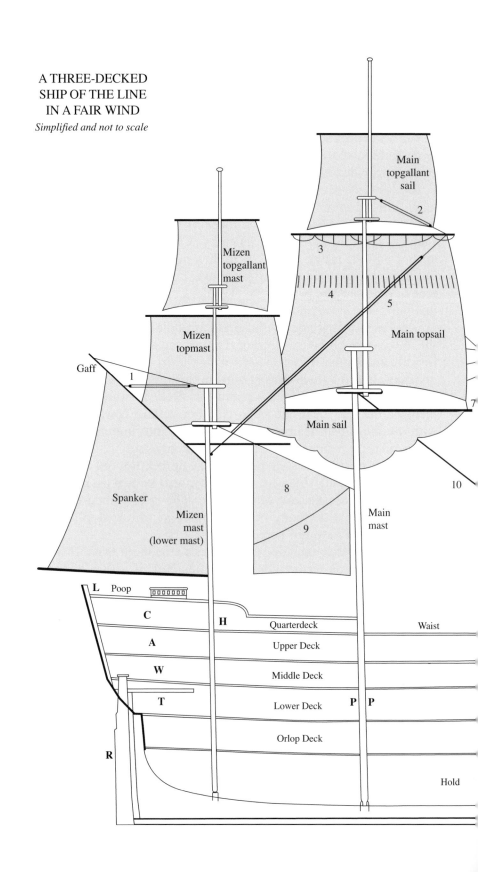

A THREE-DECKED
SHIP OF THE LINE
IN A FAIR WIND
Simplified and not to scale

Main
topgallant
sail

2

Mizen
topgallant
mast

3

Mizen
topmast

4

5

Gaff

1

Main topsail

7

Main sail

Spanker

8

10

Mizen
mast
(lower mast)

9

Main
mast

L Poop

C

H

Quarterdeck

Waist

A

Upper Deck

W

Middle Deck

T

Lower Deck

P P

Orlop Deck

R

Hold

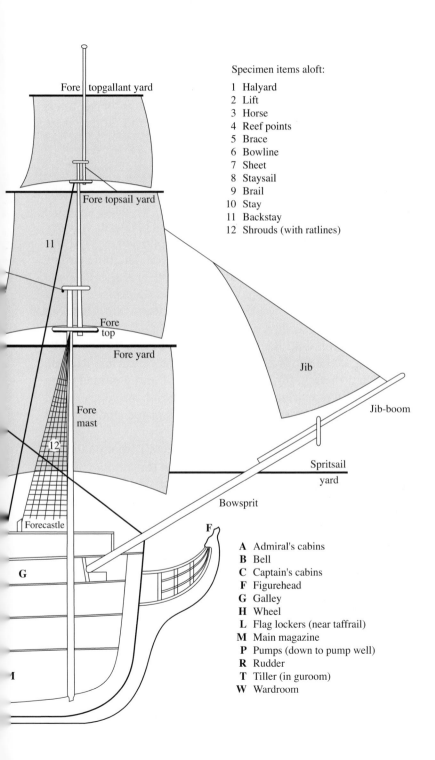

Fore | topgallant yard

Specimen items aloft:

1 Halyard
2 Lift
3 Horse
4 Reef points
5 Brace
6 Bowline
7 Sheet
8 Staysail
9 Brail
10 Stay
11 Backstay
12 Shrouds (with ratlines)

Fore topsail yard

11

Fore
top

Fore yard

Jib

Fore
mast

Jib-boom

12

Spritsail
yard

Forecastle

Bowsprit

F

G

A Admiral's cabins
B Bell
C Captain's cabins
F Figurehead
G Galley
H Wheel
L Flag lockers (near taffrail)
M Main magazine
P Pumps (down to pump well)
R Rudder
T Tiller (in guroom)
W Wardroom

the signal parties worked and flag lockers were positioned by the taffrail.

Ships carried several boats. Ships of the line typically carried a launch, a barge, a pinnace, two cutters and a jolly boat. Gigs and other boats were sometimes carried. Boats were equipped for rowing and also sailing. They were used to convey officers and men, carry stores, attack enemy shipping and sometimes to tow their ship. Most boats were stowed on booms between the gangways and some were suspended from davits aft.

The fore mast was well forward, the main mast amidships was the tallest and the mizen mast towards the stern was the shortest. Each mast comprised a lower mast, topmast and a topgallant mast. A lower mast took the weight of the lower yard and supported a platform called the top, above which rose the lower masthead. The bottom few feet of the topmast were positioned parallel to and just ahead of the lower masthead. Above was the topgallant mast and pole, made from a single piece of timber. The bowsprit and its extension the jib-boom projected forward and upwards from the head.

Yards were spars extending the heads of various sails. Their middle section was known as the slings and the ends as the yardarms. Rigging at the slings hoisted these yards, took their weight and confined them close to the mast. Men working on the yard stood on ropes called horses. Upper yards, unlike lower yards, were hoisted and lowered according to the sail set.

The lowest major sails were the courses (fore sail, main sail and mizen), above which on each mast were a topsail, a topgallant (usually pronounced t'gallant) sail and in light winds a royal. The upper edge of a square sail was the head, the sides called leeches, the lower edge the foot and lower corners the clues. Courses and topsails had one or more reef bands sewn across the width of the sail containing many reef points made of flat braided cordage hanging down on both sides of the sail. The area of sail set could be reduced in strong wind by taking some of it in by tying the reef points around the yard. A bolt rope was sewn on the edges of sails to prevent ripping. Cringles were small loops worked into the bolt rope for securing lines working the sail. Tackles and lines leading down to the clues and cringles were used to haul the sail towards the yard so that it could be reefed, furled to the yard with gaskets or brailed for temporary convenience. Studdingsails (or stunsails) could be set in light winds like wings alongside courses, topsails and topgallants on the fore and main masts.

There were also fore and aft sails. Staysails and jibs were hung from a stay. The aftermost sail was the mizen, which had its head laced to a spar called a gaff rigged diagonally aft of the mast. Alternatively, a driver or spanker was hung from a gaff and also extended at the foot by a boom.

Standing rigging supported the masts. Lower and upper masts were supported by stays led forward and downwards from the masthead. Shrouds ran down from the masthead on both sides. Ratlines were horizontal ropes crossing the shrouds to form ladders for the men to climb the rigging; it was usual to climb the weather shrouds because the wind blew them towards and not away from the rigging. Backstays providing additional support for upper masts ran down to the channels or elsewhere.

Fore and main sails, topsails, topgallants and their yards had prominent items of rigging. Upper yards were hoisted by halyards reeved through a sheave hole in the mast. Lifts keeping the yards horizontal were either single ropes or a tackle between the yardarm and masthead, where they were reeved through a block and led down to the deck. Braces enabled the yard to be turned to catch the wind. Most braces had a rope between the yardarm and a block several feet aft through which the brace itself was reeved and doubled aft with one end secured aloft and the running part led down to the deck. Bowlines kept the windward leech well forward when sailing into the wind; each had one bowline and several short bowline bridles between the bowline and cringles in the bolt rope. Sheets or tacks kept the clues extended.

The closest that a square-rigged vessel could sail to the wind was about six points, when she was said to be close-hauled. A square sail could be thrown aback and thus pressed against the mast if the wind was only one point ahead of the yard. Sails were often backed to reduce speed quickly. A ship could be brought to by having one topsail filled and another backed. A ship beating to windward by making a zig-zag course changed tack by tacking or wearing. Tacking was quicker, reduced the extent to which she fell off to leeward and involved turning her head into the wind. Wearing could be undertaken in rougher weather, put less strain on the rigging and turned the ship's head away from the wind. A vessel rigged fore and aft could sail slightly closer to the wind.

There was usually only one elderly admiral of the fleet, whose age precluded active service. Admirals, vice-admirals and rear-admirals served at sea and some as commanders-in-chief of the various naval stations. Their ranks were subdivided to reflect an obsolete fleet of three squadrons: the centre or red as the senior, the van or white next and the rear or blue as the junior. Amongst the able flag officers were three of exceptional talent: Nelson as the finest fighting admiral, St Vincent for general efficiency at sea and Middleton (later Lord Barham) for service ashore.

Captains, who were generally known as post captains, commanded all rated ships. They could be promoted to the temporary post of commodore. A captain of the fleet was a captain or rear-admiral serving as chief of staff to a commander-in-chief. A flag-captain commanded a flagship and was often a relatively junior captain. Commanders had charge of sloops and some other unrated vessels.

Lieutenants were the most junior rank of commissioned officer. Most seventy-fours had five, frigates usually had three and sloops typically one. Seniority on board each ship except flagships of commanders-in-chief was determined by the dates of their commissions: the most senior was the first lieutenant, the next was the second lieutenant and so on. The first lieutenant was the second-in-command. Lieutenants served as officers of the watch on board rated ships and commanded many unrated vessels.

Warrant officers were the specialist officers. The four most senior were of wardroom rank and were the master (responsible for navigation), the surgeon, the purser (who had charge of food, clothing and some other stores) and the chaplain. The standing officers were the gunner, carpenter and boatswain (responsible for the rigging and ensuring that the men worked ship efficiently); they had often risen from the lower deck.

Various embryonic officers messed in the cockpit on the orlop deck. They included master's mates and midshipmen. The former were the more senior and the latter were more numerous. Assistant surgeons and the captain's clerk also messed in the cockpit.

Commissioned and certain other officers usually wore a blue cloth coat, white cloth waistcoat, white breeches, white stockings, buckled black shoes and had a cocked bicorne (two-cornered) hat with a black Hanoverian rosette.

The generic term lower deck embraced lesser warrant officers, most petty officers, men and boys. Most messed and slept in hammocks on the lower deck. Lesser warrant officers included the sailmaker. Petty officers included boatswain's mates, captains of each of the three tops and quartermasters. Other men were rated according to skill and experience as an able seaman, ordinary seaman or landman. Men on watch had designations such as topmen, who were prime seamen working the ship aloft. Foreigners were often present, many boys not yet in their teens served and a few women entered in disguise. The lower deck had no prescribed uniform, although clothing known as slops issued by the purser ensured a degree of uniformity.

Pressing consisted of taking a man against his will and often by force to serve in the navy; it was the main method of recruitment. The activities of individual ships' companies were augmented by the creation in 1793 of the Impress Service. The most lucrative operations were usually at sea, with pressing also taking place in ports and roadsteads and on land. Persons aged between 18 and 55 who used the sea could be pressed. Exemptions included some officers of merchant-men and other seafarers, bearers of documents called protections issued by various authorities, foreigners unless they married a British subject and harvesters duly certified by their parish.

Marines were carried on board rated ships and sloops but not on all smaller vessels. Ranks and uniforms were similar to the army. A captain, who was of equivalent rank to a naval lieutenant, commanded the marines on board ships of the line. There was no conscription and bounties were offered as inducement to enlist. Soldiers sometimes served on board in place of marines during the Revolutionary Wars.

Prize money was paid to officers and men of those ships in sight when enemy ships, including merchantmen, were captured. The division of prize money was based upon several bands giving more money to officers and less to the lower deck. Large sums could be won by ships' companies in a single action. Hopes of prize money raised morale and helped recruitment. One lieutenant spent some of his prize money on gold chains and topaz crosses for his sisters, one of whom, the novelist Jane Austen, was somewhat concerned at his generosity and wrote to the other that she would write to thank and reproach him for his gift.

Disease caused over half of all deaths. Yellow fever and malaria were both borne by mosquitoes. The worst epidemics of yellow fever were in the West Indies: some ships lost over 100 men from yellow fever within months. Typhus was associated with rats, lice, overcrowding, inadequate ventilation and dirty clothing; it was the most prevalent fever on the Channel station.

Accidents due to nautical causes resulted in fewer deaths than disease but still more than ship disasters or enemy action. In a typical year a few hundred men drowned after falling overboard or falling from aloft onto the deck. Stormy weather or intoxication doubtless led to a high proportion of these accidents.

The third largest cause of death was that of ship disaster. The majority of ship losses were due to their being wrecked. Causes included storms, uncharted rocks, inaccurate charts, and making insufficient allowance for a strong ebb tide. Some ships were presumed to have foundered, a few small vessels sank after a collision, and several were lost due to fire or explosion.

Remarkably few casualties and ships lost were due to enemy action. Amongst the skills required of a surgeon was that of amputating limbs quickly under appalling conditions. Prisoners of war during the Revolutionary Wars were usually exchanged, whereas those captured during the Napoleonic Wars were usually held in fortress towns in north-east France.

THE BATTLE OF TRAFALGAR

Invasion Threat and 1805 Naval Campaign

The background to the Battle of Trafalgar involved the French invasion threat posed to Britain from 1803 to 1805, which was comparable to those from Spain in 1588 and Germany in 1940. There had been earlier, but less acute, invasion scares during the Revolutionary Wars.

Expeditious arrangements were undertaken at around the time of the renewal of war in 1803 to increase the number of British ships at sea. Priority had to be given to the Channel Fleet under Admiral William Cornwallis, which blockaded the French fleet in Brest. This was an often monotonous but nonetheless vital role. The next most important fleet was the Mediterranean Fleet, the commander-in-chief of which was Vice-Admiral Lord Nelson. His flagship was the *Victory*, 100, Captain Thomas Hardy. Ships were fitted out in home ports and pressing was undertaken to recruit men to serve. One successful operation was led by Captain Bowen, who landed marines at Gosport on the pretence of going to quell a mutiny at Haslar, drew a large crowd, closed the bridge and had many men pressed as they returned already disappointed at not having seen an eagerly anticipated fight.

The regular army, a new reserve army, the militia and numerous volunteer associations provided military defence. Fear of invasion encouraged many to join the colours, and the success of the army in Egypt in 1801 helped recruitment. A third of a million men enlisted in the various forces by early September 1803. Amongst those ready to fight was the future Sir Walter Scott, who practised swordsmanship by slashing at turnips placed on poles on the beach at Musselburgh.

The traditional method of beacons to warn of any invasion attempt was revived to augment other available methods. Had an invasion been attempted during daytime, hay would have been wetted and set alight to give the warning. Income tax was reintroduced in 1803 at the rate of a shilling in the pound over £150. Cartoonists ridiculed Bonaparte and drew upon the corpulent figure of John Bull as embodying British resolve. Patriotic broadsheets, songs and plays increased the fervour. Children were told that Boney ate naughty people and that they should keep quiet lest he pass by and hear them. There were a number of false alarms suggesting that the French had landed.

The French were not yet ready. The invasion date was postponed first to later dates during, and subsequently after, 1803. Bonaparte gradually amended his plans upon realising that the French fleet would have to be involved. 1804 witnessed the steady increase in the French invasion flotilla being prepared in Boulogne and other ports north and south of Cape Griz Nez. The flotilla comprised several standard classes of vessels. Ship-rigged *prames* were manned by 38 sailors, carried over 100 soldiers and mounted twelve 24-pounders. There were two classes of gun-vessels, one consisting of brigs and the other of schooners and luggers; both carried about 100 troops and many carried some horses. Schuyt-rigged *péniches*, which were undecked, carried a crew of five, 60 troops and a small mortar. These vessels were both transports and landing craft, and therefore not ideal in either role; the larger were unsuitable for landing and the smaller were unseaworthy. St Vincent, whilst First Lord and as such the government minister responsible for the navy, asserted that he did not claim that the French could not come, but only that they could not come by sea.

Britain took countermeasures. Flying squadrons prowled the Channel and undertook some operations against the invasion flotilla. Later, Martello towers were built to guard the more vulnerable stretches of coast and the Royal Military Canal was constructed to isolate the coast around Dungeness and Romney Marsh.

Pitt, whose recent public service had included that of colonel of the Cinque Ports Volunteers, succeeded Addington as prime minister in May 1804. He had resigned in 1801 due to disagreement with the king over the issue of Catholic emancipation. Addington's competence could not overcome the fact that Pitt was the dominant politician of the era.

Spanish activities had become of increasing concern to Britain. Her status as a neutral moved towards that of a covert ally of France. The British government decided to seize the Spanish treasure ships as they returned from South America. A squadron met the Spanish frigates, laden with treasure, off Cadiz on 5th October 1804. One exploded and the other three surrendered. This action prompted Spain to declare war on Britain in December. Her fleet was henceforth able to support the French fleet, stretching British resources even further. Vice-Admiral Sir John Orde was sent with a squadron to cruise off Cadiz.

The Emperor Napoleon, as Bonaparte had become, revised in 1805 his earlier plans to give France naval superiority in the Channel prior to the proposed invasion of England. Back in July 1804, he had written, "Let us be masters of the Channel for six hours and we are masters of the world." There had already been a false start in January 1805 when the Toulon fleet and Rochefort squadron escaped; they failed to unite and returned to port respectively after three days and in May. The gist of his scheme henceforth was for the French squadrons to escape, congregate in the West Indies, return together to Europe and sail up the Channel. Vice-Admiral Villeneuve was to escape from Toulon, free the Cadiz squadron and sail to the West Indies, where he would join with the Brest fleet under Ganteaume and possibly the Rochefort squadron also. The Brest fleet was to sail, raise the blockade of Ferrol and release French and Spanish ships there, sail to the West Indies and meet Villeneuve.

Villeneuve escaped from Toulon on 29th March 1805, passed through the Straits of Gibraltar and anchored in the Bay of Cadiz, where the Spanish squadron stood out to join him. Cadiz had been blockaded by Orde's small squadron, which was no match for Villeneuve's force. Orde suspected that the enemy intended to proceed to Brest and sailed north to join the Channel Fleet. Villeneuve, however, sailed for the West Indies.

Meanwhile, a scandal forced the resignation of Melville as First Lord. The able and experienced 78-year-old Admiral Sir Charles Middleton, elevated to the peerage as Lord Barham, became First Lord of the Admiralty. Although the Whig politician Creevey labelled Barham a superannuated Methodist, the wisdom of his selection was to be proved during the next few months.

Nelson heard enough to suggest that Villeneuve had probably sailed for the West Indies. He therefore left Rear-Admiral Sir Richard Bickerton in charge of the Mediterranean station and set sail with ten ships of the line in pursuit of Villeneuve's 18 ships of the line.

The French fleet arrived off Martinique on 14th May and Nelson anchored off Barbados on 4th June. Although Nelson did not meet his opponent, his relentless chase drove Villeneuve from the West Indies. Britain's colonies had been preserved and any prospect of Villeneuve lingering long enough to combine with another French force had been foiled. Nelson left Antigua on 13th June to return to Europe, having sent the *Curieux* brig ahead of him with despatches. She sighted the French fleet during her passage and on her return provided the Admiralty with this additional intelligence. Nelson arrived in Gibraltar Bay on 19th July.

The *Curieux*'s commander arrived at the Admiralty on 8th July. Barham's reaction to the intelligence provided was to concentrate upon the largest single enemy force at sea whilst keeping Admiral Cornwallis's fleet at its critical station off Brest. Vice-Admiral Collingwood was off Cadiz with his squadron and it was known that Nelson was returning. Barham planned for the possibility of Villeneuve making for Ferrol by ordering the squadron blockading Rochefort to join Vice-Admiral Sir Robert Calder, who was blockading Ferrol. Calder's combined force of 15 ships of the line was then to cruise 100 miles off Cape Finisterre, Spain's north-western point, to await Villeneuve. The French squadron in Rochefort was therefore able to sail on 16th July.

Calder arrived off Cape Finisterre on 19th July and fell in with Villeneuve's ships on 22nd July to the north-west of Cape Finisterre. It was not until the fog lifted somewhat that the Franco-Spanish fleet of 20 ships of the line was sighted. A battle was fought for the most part at long range and in poor visibility. Two of Villeneuve's ships, having dropped to leeward, surrendered.

Calder did nothing during the following two days to renew the action and by the evening of 24th July, the fleets had lost sight of each other. Villeneuve's ships anchored in Vigo Bay before a south-wester drove Calder away and thus allowed the French to reach Ferrol without having to fight. In early August, Calder realised that there was a total of 29 French and Spanish ships of the line in Ferrol and Corunna, so he raised the blockade and joined Cornwallis on 14th August. Nelson arrived off Ushant on 15th August, the *Victory* left that evening to sail for Portsmouth and anchored at Spithead on 18th August.

News of Calder's limited success caused a public outcry. He asked for a court-martial, which sat in December and ordered that he be severely reprimanded for his failure to renew the action on 23rd and 24th July. Perhaps the best comment upon the criticism heaped upon the hapless Calder came from Captain Infernet of the *Intrépide*, who was captured at Trafalgar and expressed the view that, "It is very well for you gentlemen that you can feel justified in finding fault with an admiral who, when in command of 15 sail of the line, fights a battle with 20, because he only makes two of them prizes."

Events in August posed further threats to Britain. Villeneuve sailed from Ferrol on 9th August, the day that Calder had raised the blockade thereof, hoping to fall in with the Rochefort squadron and then sail for Brest or the Channel. On 17th August, Cornwallis detached Calder with 18 ships of the line to Ferrol. Thereby splitting his fleet whilst this large Franco-Spanish fleet was at sea provided Villeneuve with the opportunity to fight either Cornwallis or Calder on favourable numerical terms. Villeneuve heard false reports of 25 British ships of the line, decided to keep to the south and on 20th August entered Cadiz.

The French fleet at Brest seldom took an active part in the 1805 campaign. The concept of a close blockade of Brest had been reintroduced by St Vincent following his appointment to command the Channel Fleet in 1800, and when Cornwallis succeeded him he continued this policy. On 20th and 21st August, Ganteaume took his fleet out beyond the Goulet so on 22nd August Cornwallis's fleet stood in to attack. During the brief engagement that followed, which involved only a few ships and a handful of casualties, it became apparent that the French were not prepared to fight beyond the range of their shore batteries. The British ships therefore wore and stood out to sea. Had Ganteaume put to sea he could have combined with other French ships to provide concentration of force. Both Cornwallis's readiness to attack and the tightness of the blockade by the Channel Fleet, which played such an important role throughout the campaign, stifled the threat.

The Third Coalition, an alliance between Britain, Russia, Austria and several other countries became effective in August 1805. Britain agreed to pay a subsidy to both Austria and Russia. Towards the end of the month, the main French army was therefore ordered by Napoleon to march from its encampments on the Channel coast to the upper Danube. Napoleon hoped to defeat Austria's army before Russia's army arrived in central Europe.

The Weeks Before the Battle

Nelson had established himself as Britain's ablest fighting sea officer during the previous decade and his pursuit of Villeneuve to the West Indies had caught the public imagination. His rise to fame started whilst commanding the *Agamemnon*, 64, in the Mediterranean from

1793 to 1796. During this period Nelson lost the use of his right eye due to a wound inflicted during the capture of Corsica. At the Battle of Cape St Vincent in 1797 he left the line of battle on his own initiative to thwart the attempt of the two parts of the larger Spanish fleet to unite and he led boarding parties onto two enemy ships. A few months later his right arm was amputated after being struck by grape shot during an unsuccessful action on the island of Tenerife. Nelson commanded the British force at the Battle of the Nile in 1798 when 11 out of 13 anchored French ships of the line were captured or destroyed. At the Battle of Copenhagen in 1801 he led part of Parker's fleet into action against the Danish line of moored vessels and fought until the Danes surrendered.

Nelson's paramount attributes were his military skills and his rapport with people. He sought to annihilate the enemy, possessed an excellent strategic appreciation, was innovative in his tactics, combined a simple basic plan with clear instructions, appreciated that the uncertainties of action might require amendment thereto and gave his captains discretion to act on their own initiative within the concept of the overall plan. He recognised the importance of concentration of force, calculated risks with accuracy, and knew how and when to seize the initiative. The admirals and captains who fought with him were infected with his zeal and officers and men both revered and were inspired by him. The civilian population had the utmost confidence in him. The Earl of Minto, who knew him well, wrote of Nelson that, "He is in many points a really great man, in others, a baby." Human weaknesses included his love affair with Emma Hamilton, ruthlessness and vanity.

At 5 am on 2nd September 1805 Captain Henry Blackwood of the *Euryalus* frigate arrived at Nelson's home at Merton with news of Villeneuve's movements. The admiral had already risen and upon meeting Blackwood exclaimed that, "I am sure you bring me news of the French and Spanish fleets, and I think I shall yet have to beat them."

Over the following days, Nelson met Pitt at Downing Street and Barham at the Admiralty. Expectations were running high that the enemy would sail from Cadiz either pursuant to orders or due to lack of provisions there. It was agreed that Nelson would return to resume command of the Mediterranean station, which was extended to include the Atlantic approach to the Straits of Gibraltar and thus the fleet off Cadiz. Whilst at the Colonial Office, Nelson met by chance the then

Major-General Sir Arthur Wellesley (the future Duke of Wellington); it was the only time that they met. He awaited with concern for confirmation that there would be sufficient copies for all his ships of Home Popham's unofficial *Marine Vocabulary*, a code book of signals that enhanced signalling potential.

Personal matters also occupied Nelson's attention. His famous love affair with Lady Hamilton, the daughter of a Cheshire blacksmith, had started whilst her husband, Sir Edward Hamilton, was the British ambassador to the Kingdom of the Two Sicilies. The age gap between the Hamiltons was 35 years whereas Nelson was only eight years older than Emma. The three lived together until Sir Edward's death. The only child of the affair was their daughter Horatia, who was born in 1801. Shortly before he left their home at Merton for the last time, Nelson and Emma took communion together and exchanged gold rings.

Nelson left Merton on 13th September and arrived at Portsmouth the following morning. He walked down to the beach at Southsea, where a crowd had collected. Such was their manifest affection towards him that Nelson was moved to exclaim to Hardy, "I had their huzzas before - I have their hearts now!" He embarked on board the *Victory*, which together with the *Euryalus* sailed down the Channel. They were joined by the *Ajax* and *Thunderer* off the Lizard. Beyond the Scillies they met the frigate taking the ill Bickerton back to England. Instructions had gone ahead that upon joining the fleet Nelson was not to be given the salute due to a commander-in-chief since he did not wish for his arrival to be known to the enemy. The *Victory* joined the fleet on 28th September.

One of Nelson's first duties involved orders to recall Calder to stand trial. With remarkable generosity, Nelson ignored his orders to send Calder home in a frigate but instead acceded to Calder's request that he be allowed to remain aboard his flagship. Arrangements were made for those captains willing to give evidence at the trial to return home to do so. It was for this reason that during the forthcoming battle the *Ajax* and *Thunderer* were both commanded by their first lieutenants.

Less than a month remained before the Battle of Trafalgar was fought. The ships of the British fleet came from a variety of commands. Only a few of them had served under Nelson in the Mediterranean, blockading Toulon and chasing Villeneuve to the West Indies; their captains and these ships Nelson knew well. Collingwood's squadron had arrived off Cadiz in the summer and had been reinforced by

Bickerton's ships on 22nd August. The largest single contingent in the Trafalgar fleet were those ships that arrived on 30th August under Calder. Nelson himself arrived on 28th September with the *Victory*, *Ajax* and *Thunderer*. Finally, a few ships were sent out from England, including the *Agamemnon*, 64, captained by Sir Edward Berry. As recently as August, Berry had written to Nelson in an endeavour to obtain a command; it seems that Nelson's influence had succeeded. On her way to join the fleet the *Agamemnon* had had a dramatic escape from the Rochefort squadron. The last of the ships to arrive that would fight at Trafalgar was the *Africa*, 64; she joined on 14th October.

Nelson engendered his personal spirit throughout the fleet, quickly getting to know those captains hitherto unfamiliar to him. He invited half his captains to dinner on 29th September, the day after his arrival, and the other half the following day. The former date happened to be Nelson's forty-seventh birthday. One captain new to Nelson was George Duff of the *Mars*, who as soon as 1st October wrote to his wife that, "He certainly is the pleasantest Admiral I ever served under." In a later letter to his wife dated 10th October he commented, "He is so good and pleasant a man, that we all wish to do what he likes, without any kind of orders."

Nelson and Collingwood had known each other since their early careers in the West Indies, when they had sketched each other and Collingwood had succeeded Nelson in command of two vessels. The *Victory*'s captain and chaplain provided Nelson with exceptional support. Captain Thomas Hardy had been Nelson's favoured flag-captain for some years and by this stage he was serving also as an unofficial captain of the fleet. The Rev Alexander Scott had developed an extra-curricular aptitude for languages whilst at Cambridge and upon joining the navy also undertook confidential, secretarial and intelligence work.

Of particular importance was Nelson's promulgation of his intended manner of fighting a fleet action, which was formally distributed under the title Secret Memorandum. The order of sailing was to be the order of battle, with the fleet divided into two parallel lines plus an advanced squadron of several of the fastest two-deckers. Nelson's line was to cut through near the centre of the enemy line and the second-in-command's line was to cut through beginning from the twelfth ship from the enemy's rear. His objective was to ensure victory before the van could support the centre and rear. Upon explaining his plans to his captains, he observed that, as he wrote to Emma, "when I came to explain to them the 'Nelson touch', it was like an electric shock. Some shed tears, all approved - 'It was new - it was singular - it was simple!' " Remarkably, Villeneuve either had foreseen or knew of Nelson's plan of attack.

Other issues also preoccupied Nelson. Thus he arranged to help one of his captains whose son, a lieutenant, had run away with an opera dancer from Malta and was feared to be in prison for debt.

Ships' sides were painted in a style that became known as the 'Nelson chequer'. This consisted of the side being painted yellow with a broad black line between each row of gun ports, the lids of which were also painted black.

It is natural to think of the events of October 1805 as being a continuation of the summer's campaign. In a sense they were, and it was the events of the summer that explained why the various fleets and squadrons were stationed as they were. However, the earlier events had been concerned primarily with the intended invasion of Britain. The sailing of the combined Franco-Spanish fleet in October, on the other hand, had nothing to do with any invasion of Britain. The combined fleet sailed because it was carrying troops to Italy with a view to combining with French armies there in an attempt to capture Sicily, Britain's long-standing but vulnerably located ally.

Napoleon's orders of 18th September to Vice-Admiral Rosily, who was to supersede Villeneuve, for him to sail included the option not to risk battle on unfavourable terms. Although he became aware that the fleet blockading Cadiz had been greatly strengthened, the emperor did not countermand his orders; perhaps he was distracted by his forthcoming military campaign. Villeneuve summoned a council of war, which met on board his flagship the *Bucentaure* on 8th October and decided to await either the blockading fleet being driven off station by bad weather or detaching ships to protect trade. As it happened, Nelson had already detached a squadron under Rear-Admiral Louis to revictual: five ships left the fleet on 3rd October and the *Donegal* was detached later to obtain water. Nelson may not have expected Villeneuve to sail as soon as he did and hoped that Louis and these ships would return in time for the anticipated battle. Anyway, when Villeneuve learned that four British ships of the line had sailed east from Gibraltar with a convoy and two others were in the Bay, he concluded that he would not be able to encounter the British fleet with fewer ships.

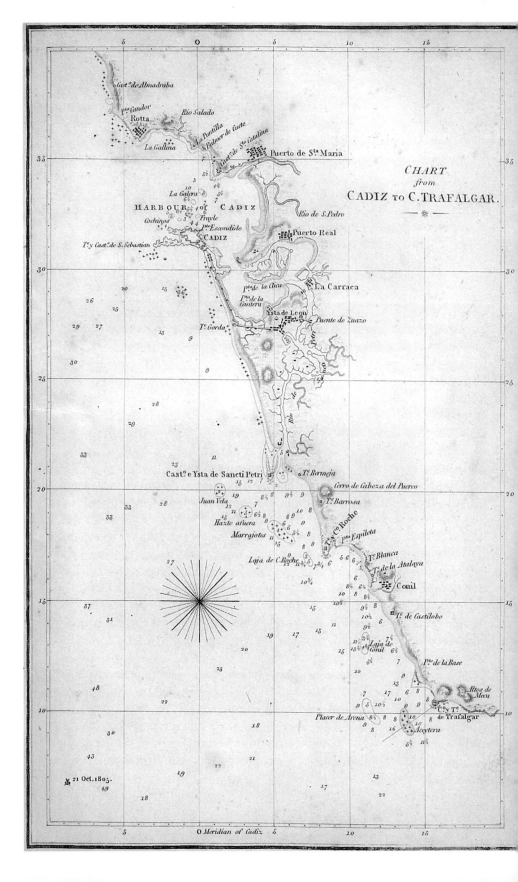

CHART
from
CADIZ TO C. TRAFALGAR.

Cast.º de Almadraba
P.ta Candor
Rotta
Rio Salado
La Pastilla
La Palmer de Cueto
Cast.º de S.ta Catalina
Puerto de S.ta Maria
La Gallina

35

3
10
La Galera
6½
4½
5½
Cochinos
Frayle
P.to Escondido
CADIZ
T.e y Cast.º de S. Sebastian
HARBOUR of CADIZ
Rio de S.Pedro
Puerto Real

30

20
15
36
26
25
29
27
13
T.e Gorda
9
30
9

P.to de la Clica
P.to de la Cantera
Ysta de Leon
La Carraca
Puente de Zuazo

25

28
29
33

23
11
Cast.º e Ysta de Sancti Petri
T.e Beringa
15 12 7
Cerro de Cabeza del Puerco
28
Juan Vela
19
12
7
8½ 9½ 9
11
6½ 6
15
8 8
T.e Barrosa
33 33
28
Haxte afuera
6
8 9 10 8
Marrajotes
4 6
5½
T.e Roche
15
5½ 8
P.ta Espileta
Laja de C. Roche
3 6
6
T.e Blanca
27
12
7 2¾ 6
T.e de la Atalaya
10¾
6
Conil
8½ 8
10
8 8½

20

37
31
15
10½ 8
T.e de Castilobo
19 17
11
9½ 6
15
9½
20
8 3
Laja de Conil
15 13½ 6¾
25
5½
7
P.ta de la Base
10
13
Altos de Meca
18
7 17 10 8 8
22
7 5 10½ 8 8 8
C.º y T.e de Trafalgar
30
Placer de Arena
9 8 8 10
8
Accytera
43 21
5½ 11
18
19
22
17
13
22
X 21 Oct. 1805.
49
18

15

10

35

30

25

20

15

10

5   0   5   10   15

5   0 Meridian of Cadiz   5   10   15

The remaining factors in Villeneuve's decision to sail were personal. He knew that Napoleon was furious with him due to his lack of success during the summer. He had surmised correctly that Rosily had been appointed to replace him and heard that he had reached Madrid.

Vice-Admiral Gravina was the senior Spanish officer in the fleet. Although he was senior to Villeneuve, the combined fleet was under the latter's command because the 1804 alliance had stipulated that any such fleet should be led by a French officer. Gravina had been under secret orders from his government not to enter Brest, both to avoid leaving Spain's coasts unprotected and also to thwart any successful attempt to invade Britain.

Most of the British fleet lay 40 or 50 miles to the west as a precaution against being driven through the Straits of Gibraltar by a westerly gale and enabling the enemy to take advantage of a ship of wind to the east to escape into the Atlantic before the British fleet could resume its station. In the event of a fresh easterly breeze, the fleet would beat up to Cadiz. Three ships of the line acted as links between the fleet and Blackwood's frigates and smaller vessels stationed closest inshore watching Cadiz.

Villeneuve ordered a squadron of nine ships of the line and three frigates under Rear-Admiral Magon to sea. It began to weigh anchor at 7 am on 19th October. At 6.04 am the *Sirius* signalled to the *Euryalus*, "Enemy have their topsail yards hoisted." At 7 am the *Sirius* signalled, again to the *Euryalus*, "Enemy's ships are coming out of port." Having cleared the entrance to Cadiz, the wind dropped and Magon's squadron lay becalmed but under no immediate danger since the main blockading fleet was well out to sea. Blackwood's signals had reported events to Nelson, who ordered a general chase to the south-east. It was not until the early afternoon that a west-south-westerly breeze enabled the Frenchmen to stand northwards, shadowed by Blackwood's frigates. Some British officers were fearful that the enemy was merely making a feint and would return to Cadiz.

On the morning of 20th October, the British fleet was south-west of Cape Trafalgar on the Spanish coast between Cadiz and the Straits of Gibraltar. The British fleet thus barred the entrance to the Mediterranean and was well positioned to rejoin Louis's ships had

---

A contemporary chart of the coast from Cadiz to Cape Trafalgar. The location of the battle is marked near the south-west corner.

the *Weazle* sloop, despatched by Blackwood, fallen in with them. At 6.20 am it wore and at 8 am it hove to.

Meanwhile, Villeneuve decided to sail with his entire fleet. It therefore weighed anchor and left Cadiz during the morning of 20th October. The combined fleet's manoeuvres during the following hours as it grappled with the weather demonstrated a lack of cohesion. The enemy's departure was duly signalled to Nelson, whose fleet remained well to the south of the Franco-Spanish fleet throughout the day. At 10.30 am, the British fleet sailed west-north-west and at 4 pm it sailed northwards. At 5 pm, the *Naiad* reported that the combined fleet was sailing south. At 8.30 pm, the British fleet wore and stood south-south-west.

The Battle

The morning of Monday 21st October dawned with a hazy sun, the sea smooth and a swell coming in from the Atlantic. At 6.10 am Nelson signalled his fleet to form order of sailing in two columns, at 6.22 am to prepare for battle and at 6.46 am to sail due east.

The British ships cleared for action. Some steps may have been taken previously. Gun decks were prepared by making them long open spaces from bows to stern. Bulkheads were removed and furniture, together with unnecessary pillars and ladders, were taken below. Animals in the manger were often slaughtered. Some objects were thrown overboard. Either now or later the guns were unleashed and small arms were distributed. Emergency steering gear was made available. The cockpit on the orlop deck was made ready to treat casualties. In the magazine preparations were made for the supply of powder for the guns. Precautions aloft included rigging chain slings to support the lower yards and nets between the masts several feet above the decks in the hope of catching objects shot away. The Windsor chairs of the *Tonnant*'s wardroom were suspended from a rope slung aloft between the main and mizen masts.

Villeneuve had expected to encounter a somewhat smaller British fleet. His quandary on the morning of 21st October was the choice between continuing to sail south-east towards the Straits of Gibraltar in accordance with the object of his mission or sailing back towards Cadiz. He chose the latter course, probably due to a desire to keep his fleet together for the forthcoming battle. At 8 am, he signalled to his fleet to wear together and form line of battle on the port tack. This resulted in the battle being fought with the combined fleet sailing in a northerly direction with Cadiz bearing to leeward on its starboard bow, and thus positioned advantageously for retreat.

The Franco-Spanish fleet now sailed in inverted order and was led by the *Neptuno*. It comprised four squadrons, each of which contained a mixture of French and Spanish ships. The Third Squadron commanded by Rear-Admiral Dumanoir Le Pelly now led. It was followed by the First Squadron led by Villeneuve. Then came the Second Squadron commanded by Vice-Admiral de Alava. Finally, the Squadron of Observation brought up the rear, its two divisions being commanded by Rear-Admiral Magon and Vice-Admiral Gravina. The Squadron of Observation, in extending the line south of the Second Squadron, obeyed Gravina's order in preference to Villeneuve's for it to stay to windward ready to support the centre. The fleet's frigates were to leeward. Although sailing north, the combined fleet formed a crescent with its centre somewhat to the east of a notional north-south line drawn between its tips. Some of those present in the British fleet suggested subsequently that this crescent formation had been merely an optical illusion but it seems that the combined fleet did create this shape.

The British fleet of 27 ships of the line consisted of three ships of 100 guns each, four of 98 guns, one of 80 guns, sixteen of 74 guns and three of 64 guns. Also present but not due to take any part in the fighting were four frigates, a cutter and a schooner. The Franco-Spanish fleet of 33 ships of the line comprised 17 French and 16 Spanish ships: four ships (all Spanish) were of 100 guns or more, six of 84 or 80 guns, twenty-two of 74 guns and one of 64 guns. It was attended by five frigates and two brigs. There was a light west-north-westerly breeze and a heavy swell from the west. Cape Trafalgar, pronounced by the Spaniards Trafflegar with emphasis on the last syllable, was distantly visible. Some Spaniards ashore were to have a distant view of the battle.

Some confusion relating to ship nomenclature merits mention. There were instances of two or even all of the nations present having ships of similar or identical names. Thus the British *Neptune*, French *Neptune* and Spanish *Neptuno* were amongst the ships of the line present. Both Britain and France had ships named *Achille* and *Swiftsure* present. It was commonplace for captured ships to retain their original name, which resulted in the *Berwick*, having been captured from Britain by France in 1795, forming part of the Franco-Spanish fleet.

The Trafalgar Fleets

British ships of the line

Franco-Spanish ships of the line

Nelson's line
Victory, 100
Téméraire, 98
Neptune, 98
Leviathan, 74
Conqueror, 74
Britannia, 100
Ajax, 74
Agamemnon, 64
Orion, 74
Minotaur, 74
Spartiate, 74
Africa, 64 (detached)

Collingwood's line
Royal Sovereign, 100
Belleisle, 74
Mars, 74
Tonnant, 80
Bellerophon, 74
Colossus, 74
Achille, 74
Revenge, 74
Defiance, 74
Dreadnought, 98
Polyphemus, 64
Swiftsure, 74
Thunderer, 74
Defence, 74
Prince, 98

Neptuno, 80 (Sp)
Scipion, 74 (Fr)
Intrépide, 74 (Fr)
Formidable, 80 (Fr)
Mont Blanc, 74 (Fr)
Duguay Trouin, 74 (Fr)
Rayo, 100 (Sp)
San Fransisco de Asis, 74 (Sp)
San Agustin, 74 (Sp)
Héros, 74 (Fr)
Santissima Trinidad, 130 (Sp)
Bucentaure, 80 (Fr)
Redoutable, 74 (Fr)
San Justo, 74 (Sp)
Neptune, 80 (Fr)
San Leandro, 64 (Sp)
Santa Ana, 112 (Sp)
Indomptable, 80 (Fr)
Fougueux, 74 (Fr)
Pluton, 74 (Fr)
Monarca, 74 (Sp)
Algésiras, 74 (Fr)
Bahama, 74 (Sp)
Montañez, 74 (Sp)
Aigle, 74 (Fr)
Swiftsure, 74 (Fr)
Argonaute, 74 (Fr)
Argonauta, 80 (Sp)
San Ildefonso, 74 (Sp)
Achille, 74 (Fr)
Principe de Asturias, 112 (Sp)
Berwick, 74 (Fr)
San Juan Nepomuceno, 74 (Sp)

Frigates and lesser vessels also present

The British fleet was formed into two straggling lines. Nelson led the weather, northern and port division and Collingwood led the lee, southern and starboard division. Nelson's line sailed with its ships more or less ahead and astern of their consorts. Collingwood signalled to his ships to form on the port line of bearing, which resulted in most of them sailing on the starboard quarter of the ship ahead. By the evening of 20th October, Duff's squadron of two-deckers had been absorbed into the rest of the fleet, probably due both to the manoeuvring during the day and the fact that Nelson's plan had originally envisaged a battle between two somewhat larger fleets. Although Collingwood's line is generally referred to as the lee division, it should be appreciated that this merely reflected the fact that his division was slightly further to leeward and therefore closer to the enemy's than Nelson's; Collingwood's division still held the weather gauge over the Franco-Spanish fleet. His flagship was the *Royal Sovereign*. The only other admiral in the British fleet was Rear-Admiral the Earl of Northesk, who flew his flag in the *Britannia*. The British frigates and smaller vessels were to the north of Nelson's line.

Nelson's tactics have received both praise for brilliance and criticism for exposing his fleet to danger by approaching the enemy in line ahead. By sailing almost at right angles to the enemy, the British ships were exposed to their fire whilst unable to bring their broadsides to bear. Nelson's tactics on the day differed somewhat to those originally drawn up. There is some basis, not least because of lines drawn on memoranda, to suggest that Nelson may have had in mind also the alternative possibility of sailing initially parallel to the enemy before cutting their line at right angles in two places.

The Battles of the Glorious First of June in 1794 and Camperdown in 1797 both help to weigh the risks involved of such an attack. In both battles, the British fleet approached the enemy at right angles, and in both instances victories were won without a single ship being lost. In the former battle, the British fleet approached in line abreast and in the latter case, in two groups of ships.

One of the key objectives was to engage quickly enough to be able to win a decisive victory on the day of battle. Cadiz and shoals were not far away, and the light wind meant that hours would elapse before any fighting. Thus Nelson had to catch the enemy as quickly as possible, and his tactics may have been modified accordingly. His problem was not whether he would beat the combined fleet but whether he could force a decisive victory.

The disadvantage was that the leading ships, most notably the *Victory* and *Royal Sovereign*, were badly damaged during the approach. But as the enemy line was cut, ship after ship fired destructive raking broadsides into the enemy with shot flying the length of the hull and inflicting many casualties and much damage. Many French and Spanish ships were never able to recover from those early raking broadsides. Nelson had assessed the risks carefully and was to be justified by the results. He would have had regard to the fact that the swell coming in from the Atlantic would make accurate shooting other than at point-blank range very difficult and that the enemy, having been shut up in port, was unused to being at sea.

The combined fleet sought action at close quarters, so as to use the many troops embarked to best effect. Its ships sailed in close albeit irregular formation. Nelson remarked frequently that they were putting a good face on it, adding, "I'll give them such a dressing as they never had before." Blackwood saw that they waited the British attack with a coolness that he was sorry to witness.

The *Victory* remained the leading ship of the weather division. This caused concern to certain officers, being well aware of the value of Nelson's life. Blackwood at some stage raised with Nelson the possibility that he hoist his flag on board the *Euryalus*, where he could observe events better and give any necessary orders. Nelson would not hear of this, giving the force of example as his reason. Blackwood suggested to Nelson the desirability of permitting one or two ships to sail ahead of the *Victory*. Nelson agreed, but when the *Téméraire* ranged up on the *Victory*'s quarter in order to pass her, Nelson hailed her and told her to stay astern.

Nelson had, earlier in the morning, made a codicil to his will asking the country to provide for Emma and Horatia, which he had witnessed by Hardy and Blackwood. Later, at about 11 am, he knelt at a table in his cabin and wrote a brief prayer:-

May the Great God, whom I worship, grant to my Country, and for the benefit of Europe in general, a great and glorious Victory; and may no misconduct in any one tarnish it; and may humanity after Victory be the predominant feature in the British Fleet. For myself, individually, I commit my life to Him who made me, and may his blessing light upon my endeavours for serving my Country faithfully. To Him I resign myself and the just cause which is entrusted to me to defend. Amen. Amen. Amen.

The light wind meant that the approach of the British fleet towards the enemy was slow. Officers and men had ample time for conversation and inner thoughts. They looked forward to glory and prize money, welcomed the prospect of action after years of dreary and arduous blockade duty, and thought of home and family. Fears of death or injury would usually have been kept unuttered. The general mood was one of high spirits, which a midshipman on the *Bellerophon* described to be as if they were preparing for a festival rather than combat. Some guns' crews chalked slogans such as 'Victory or Death' on their cannon. Hornpipes were danced and bands played tunes including 'Rule Britannia', 'Hearts of Oak' and 'Britons, Strike Home.' Captain Mansfield of the *Minotaur* addressed his men assembled on the quarterdeck from the break of the poop; they replied with cheers. Arrangements were made for early dinner and the *Bellerophon*'s captain joined the officers for a meal including cold meat, using the rudderhead as a makeshift table.

As battle neared, captains gave the order for marine drummers to 'Beat to quarters' and officers and men went to their positions. The gun port lids were opened and the guns were run out. The galley fire, if still alight, was extinguished. Sand was sprinkled on the decks to help men to retain their footing. Once within range of enemy fire, men on some ships were ordered to lie down to reduce casualties from raking shot, although officers remained standing.

Cannon were muzzle-loaded, cast of iron and had a smooth bore or calibre. The inboard end was the breech and the outer end the muzzle. The gun was mounted on a hollow wooden carriage the two sides of which were called cheeks and the four wheels called trucks. The breeching rope restrained the cannon and mitigated its recoil. One gun tackle was rigged on either side to run the gun out and a train tackle at the rear hooked to a ringbolt in the deck prevented the gun from rolling out whilst being loaded.

The carronade was a short-range gun which was lighter, shorter and required fewer hands than a cannon. A typical carriage pivoted below the muzzle, had two large pieces of wood called the slide and bed, one above the other, and had at the rear two small wheels for traversing and a vertical screw for elevation. Upon firing, the slide recoiled whilst the larger, lower bed below it did not; the vertical bolt connecting them was prone to break upon recoil.

The standard arrangement was to have the heaviest guns on the lower deck and progressively lighter guns on higher decks. Thus the *Victory*'s lower deck mounted 32-pounders, her middle deck 24-pounders and her upper deck and quarterdeck 12-pounders. She also carried two 68-pounder carronades and two 12-pounder cannon on her forecastle.

The basic cannon ball, called round shot, was a solid ball of cast iron. Grape shot consisted of nine smaller shot enclosed in a canvas bag and corded together to create a cylindrical shape the same diameter as a cannon ball. Case shot or canister shot was an anti-personnel weapon comprising a tin case filled with numerous smaller lead balls. Other types of shot were rarely used by the navy because British tactics advocated firing into an enemy's hull in preference to damaging her aloft. Double-headed shot consisted of one ball formed in two separate halves joined by a bar.

Guns were cleaned and loaded at the muzzle. A sponge was used to clean the gun after firing and a rammer to ram home the cartridge and shot; a common tool was a stiffened rope with a sponge at one end and a rammer at the other. A worm was used to remove any charge not fired and after every few discharges to help clear the chamber. The flannel cartridge filled with gunpowder was loaded first, followed by a wad, then the shot and finally a second wad. Then the cannon was run out and trained by slewing the rear of the carriage round with handspikes. Elevation was controlled by placing handspikes under the breech and adjusting a wooden wedge called a quoin. The cartridge was pricked through the vent hole near the breech with a priming iron of wire, a goose quill tube containing a paste with a composition similar to that of gunpowder was inserted down the vent hole, and priming powder from a powder horn was poured onto the pan. The gun was discharged by pulling the lanyard of the flintlock and causing a spark so that fire was conveyed down to the cartridge to create an explosion. Alternatively lit match, usually attached to a linstock, could be used. Upon firing, a cannon recoiled a few feet inboard, which assisted loading.

The cannon of a broadside were not fired simultaneously to reduce the strain on the hull. Raking fire amounted to firing upon an adversary from ahead or astern with the result that destructive shot could pass the length of the hull.

As the fleets closed, ships' companies were sent to quarters. The captain, first lieutenant, master and captain's clerk were stationed on the quarterdeck. The marine officers and some of their men were stationed on the poop; the others were distributed on the gundecks. The boatswain was on most ships in charge on the forecastle. Small

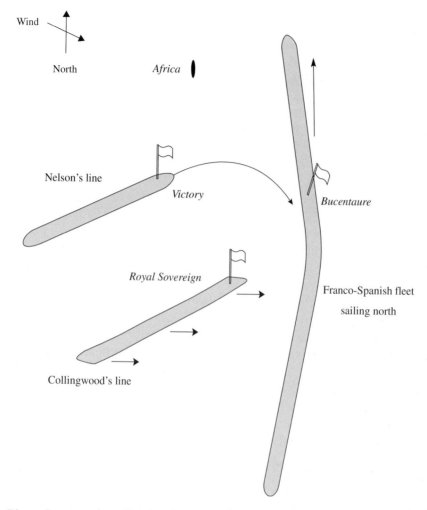

Wind

North

Africa

Nelson's line

Victory

Bucentaure

Royal Sovereign

Franco-Spanish fleet
sailing north

Collingwood's line

Plan of approach to Battle of Trafalgar – The position at about noon. The Franco-Spanish fleet sailing north whilst the British fleet sails from the west in two lines.

groups of seamen were stationed at the wheel and in the tops. Two lieutenants were usually assigned to each gundeck; the senior on each had overall control and both had direct responsibility for half the deck. Master's mates and midshipmen each supervised a few guns. Most of the men were quartered at the guns. Each gun's crew was responsible for two guns, one on each side of the ship. There was a first captain and second captain of each and others were designated as loaders, spongers, handspikemen and tackle-men. Some were liable to be summoned for other duties: boarders armed with cutlasses to board an enemy or repel boarders, sail trimmers to assist aloft, firemen to put out a fire and winchmen to man the pumps. Powder boys were allocated to fetch powder. The surgeon and his party, the chaplain and usually also the purser awaited casualties in the after cockpit. The gunner and his party were in the magazine and the carpenter and his mates waited on the orlop deck ready to plug shot holes near or below the waterline.

Whilst the fleets closed and at about 11.40 am, Nelson, who was on the poop, told Blackwood that he intended to amuse the fleet with a signal. He turned to Lieutenant John Pasco, the signal lieutenant, and instructed him to make the signal "England confides that every man will do his duty." Popham's unofficial code was used because its vocabulary enabled original messages to be sent. It seems that he had already adopted a suggestion to start it with the word 'England' instead of 'Nelson.' Pasco sought Nelson's permission to substitute the word 'expects' for 'confides' since the former word was in the signal book whereas confides would have needed to have been spelt out. The signal comprised twelve successive flag hoists to the mizen topgallant masthead, one for each of the first eight words ('England', for example, was number 253 in the code) with only 'duty' having to be spelt by means of a further four hoists. Reaction to Nelson's celebrated signal was mixed. Some of the *Ajax*'s men murmured, "Do our duty! Of course we'll do our duty" and then cheered.

Nelson's last general signal was "Engage the enemy more closely", which was signal number 16 in Howe's code and consisted of two flags. The upper flag (number 1) consisted of a blue cross on a white background and the lower flag (number 6) of three horizontal stripes of blue uppermost, white in the middle and red at the bottom. This signal was hoisted at 12.15 pm and remained flying at the main topgallant masthead until it was shot away.

Blackwood and Captain Prowse of the *Sirius* left Nelson when the admiral noticed the enemy's shot passing over the *Victory*. Nelson instructed them to tell the captains of the ships of the line that he depended upon their exertions and that if the plan of attack did not bring them into action promptly, they might do whatever they thought best provided it led them quickly and closely alongside an enemy. Nelson and Blackwood shook hands on the poop, the captain adding, "I trust, my Lord, that on my return to the *Victory*, which will be as soon as possible, I shall find your lordship well and in possession of twenty prizes." Nelson's reply was, "God bless you, Blackwood, I shall never speak to you again."

The following narrative of the battle covers the ships of Collingwood's line before turning to those in Nelson's line. The *Fougueux* opened fire upon the *Royal Sovereign* at 11.58 am and the *Royal Sovereign* cut the line ten minutes later. Collingwood's leading ships were in action well before those of Nelson; the *Victory* cut the line at about 12.45 pm. Times are known to be approximate only, not least because the logs of different ships recorded the same events at different times.

The *Royal Sovereign* was the ideal ship to lead the lee column having regard to her strength as a three-decker and the enhanced sailing qualities provided by her recently acquired copper bottom. In one sense it could be said that the king was leading his fleet into battle. The *Royal Sovereign*'s figurehead was a full-length carving of George III wearing the battle dress of a Roman emperor, with a sword at his side, a sceptre in his hand and a red cloak on his shoulders, with winged figures of Fortune and Fame on either side blowing gold trumpets.

Nelson's plan had envisaged the lee line cutting the enemy line "beginning from the twelfth ship from the rear." However, the *Royal Sovereign* sailed for the *Santa Ana*, the sixteenth ship from the rear. It may have been that the enemy line was so disorganised, with some ships abreast of each other, that Collingwood had not appreciated how many ships were astern of the *Santa Ana*.

As the *Royal Sovereign* approached, the *Santa Ana* (which was the flagship of Vice-Admiral Alava) backed her mizen topsail and the *Fougueux*, the ship immediately astern of her, made sail in a vain attempt to close the gap. Collingwood responded by ordering Rotheram, his flag-captain, to carry away the *Fougueux*'s bowsprit. The *Fougueux*, deterred, gave way and the *Royal Sovereign* cut the line, firing her port broadside into the *Santa Ana*'s stern and her starboard broadside into the *Fougueux*. Collingwood was moved to observe, "Rotheram, what would Nelson give to be here!"

The *Royal Sovereign* then ran along the lee side of the *Santa Ana*. The rival flagships were so close that their yardarms locked together. For a few minutes, the *Royal Sovereign* was virtually surrounded without any nearby support. The *Santa Ana* was on her port beam, whilst further off the *Fougueux* raked her from astern and the *San Leandro* from ahead. The *San Justo* lay on her starboard bow and the *Indomptable* on her starboard quarter. Such was the fire from these ships that those on board the *Royal Sovereign* saw enemy shot colliding with each other. Soon, however, the *Belleisle* engaged the two Frenchmen and the two flagships were left fighting together.

This part of the battle was a captain's affair rather than an admiral's, and Collingwood found himself with little to do. At some stage, perhaps now, he paced the poop munching an apple. He instructed the captain of marines to remove his men from the poop, where they were exposed to danger. Noticing a topgallant studdingsail loose he desired a lieutenant to assist him to get it in. He also talked to the men at the guns.

The scene below decks was similar to that on other ships engaged. Fire and smoke from the guns, their thunder and recoil upon being discharged, exertions as guns were run out again, shouts, occasional cheers, screams from the wounded and crashes of enemy shot were the main features as men fought in confined, crowded and dim conditions. They knew virtually nothing about events beyond those taking place in their immediate vicinity. A seaman named Sam wrote afterwards that at the start of the action he wished that he was back at Warnborough with his plough, but soon thought no more about being killed than had he been at Murrell Green Fair.

The *Santa Ana*'s fire was slackening by 2 pm. Her fore and main masts fell and she surrendered at 2.20 pm. She had fought to sufficient effect that Collingwood's flagship took virtually no further part in the battle. At 2.30 pm the *Royal Sovereign*'s main mast fell and in doing so brought down the mizen mast. Her fore mast remained standing although badly damaged. Collingwood signalled for the *Euryalus* to take the *Royal Sovereign* in tow.

The *Belleisle*, 74, Captain William Hargood, was the second ship in the lee division. It was probably no more than five minutes or so after the *Royal Sovereign* had entered the action that the *Belleisle* was engaged. By this time, there was hardly any need to shorten sail on board the *Belleisle*, such had been the effect of the fire to which she had already been exposed. The *Belleisle*'s first port broadside was fired into

---

This plan shows the crucial phase of the battle. The *Royal Sovereign* and ships to the south of her would have been in these positions at times averaging about 1 pm, and the ships to the north of her at times around 1.30 pm. British ships are still closing from the west, the van of the Franco-Spanish fleet to the north is not in action and its rear to the south has yet to be engaged.

Plan of Battle of Trafalgar at its crucial phase

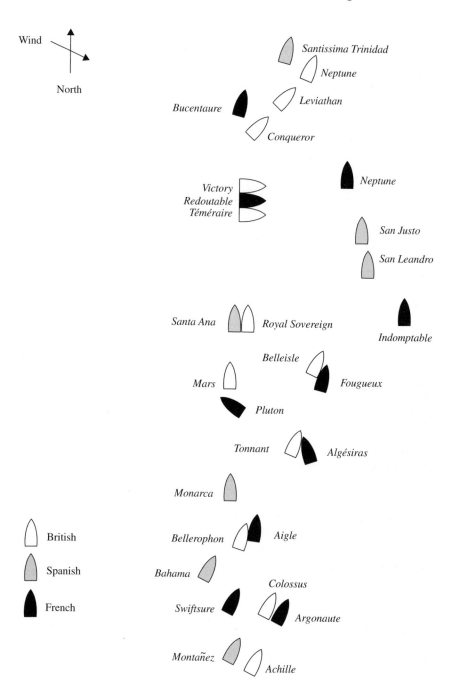

the *Santa Ana* and her starboard broadside into the *Fougueux*. The *Fougueux*'s port bow soon struck the *Belleisle*'s starboard gangway, with her fore yard over the *Belleisle*'s quarterdeck, and they remained locked together for nearly an hour. The *Indomptable* wore across the *Belleisle*'s bows, raked her and drifted away.

At 12.40 pm the *Belleisle*'s main topmast was shot away, and by 1 pm she was engaged with three ships. At 1.10 pm, the mizen mast was shot away about six feet above the poop. Soon thereafter, the *Fougueux*, having been severely mauled by the *Belleisle*, sheered off. Ten minutes or so later, however, the *Achille* passed under the *Belleisle*'s stern and subsequently stationed herself on her port quarter. The *Aigle*, having previously engaged the *Bellerophon*, soon thereafter occupied the place vacated by the *Fougueux*. The *Belleisle* was by this time totally unmanagable, having had all her sails and rigging shot away, and her fore and main masts were both in a tottering state. The main mast fell aft on the port side of the poop at 2.10 pm.

At 2.30 pm, the French *Neptune*, 80, placed herself on the starboard bow of the *Belleisle*. Soon afterwards, the *Belleisle*'s fore mast fell over the starboard bow, carrying with it the bowsprit and figurehead. At 3 pm, the *Belleisle* was still engaging the three ships already named, offering stout resistance. Welcome assistance arrived at 3.20 pm or thereabouts. The *Polyphemus* engaged the *Neptune*, the *Defiance* fought the *Aigle*, and soon afterwards the *Swiftsure* passed under the *Belleisle*'s stern, greeted her crew with three hearty cheers and engaged the *Pluton*.

The *Belleisle*'s crew were thus afforded their first respite since the action had begun, and set to work clearing the wreckage. They had been in action for over three hours. Some relieved their thirst during the battle by eating the captain's grapes that were still hung around his cabin. The Spanish *Argonauta*, 80, which had been engaged by the British *Achille*, came down near the *Belleisle* and hoisted British colours. The master, William Hudson, and Lieutenant John Owen of the marines were sent with a prize crew in the pinnace to take possession of her.

The *Belleisle* was the only British ship to be totally dismasted, and after 4 pm was taken in tow by the *Naiad*. Her reported casualties were 33 killed and 93 wounded. One fortunate seaman was discovered to breathe as he was being launched over the poop. After a week in hospital, the ball that had entered at his temple came out through his mouth.

The casualty list did not include the captain, who did not report his own wound. Hargood had been knocked down by a splinter but had refused to leave the deck. Subsequent examination revealed extensive bruising reaching from his throat down nearly as far as his waist. This injury may have been caused when netting became displaced, entangled Hargood and knocked him down. Upon getting free, and still somewhat stunned and animated, he called out, "Let them come on, I'm damned if I'll strike. No, never, to nobody whatever!" This was heard by those around him and during lulls in the action was relayed to other decks, with a cheering effect on the ship's company.

Many years later, Hargood was to receive a gift of eight bottle stands made from the *Belleisle*'s timbers. One anecdote relating to Admiral Sir William Hargood whilst commander-in-chief at Plymouth in the 1830's typifies inevitable feelings of nostalgia. A lieutenant commanding a brig sought a steamship to tow him out of the Hamoaze; Sir William retorted by observing that had he not worked out of the Hamoaze with the wind two points more against him, he would not have been at Trafalgar and advised the lieutenant to find his way to the Sound without further delay.

The third ship in the lee division was the *Mars*, 74, Captain George Duff. She hove to so as to avoid the *Santa Ana* ahead. The *Mars* shortly found herself in a perilous position with a French ship on either side, a Spanish ship on her bow and a fourth ship also within range. The *Tonnant* soon engaged two of these ships but the *Mars* received destructive fire from the *Pluton*.

Norman, the captain of marines, was on the poop and realised that a French ship, probably the *Pluton*, was getting into a position which would enable her to rake the *Mars*. He therefore went down to the quarterdeck to report this to Captain Duff. The lack of wind made it

---

(*overleaf*)

'Nelson on the Quarterdeck of the *Victory*' by W.H. Overend. Nelson is looking towards the 12-pounders on the port side of the *Victory*'s quarterdeck. Further right are Hardy, a lieutenant and a midshipman, and a marine is on the deck. On the nearer cannon, the flintlock and lanyard are visible, and a marine is holding a handspike. Guns' crews are prominent. Further forward, masts and the bowsprit can be seen. Tackles and blocks, for both rigging and guns, are visible.

impossible to alter the position of the *Mars*, and to have done so would probably have exposed her to greater danger from other ships. The two discussed whether their guns would bear on her. Duff went to the end of the quarterdeck to look over the side and then sent his aide-de-camp below with an order for the guns to be pointed further aft. Scarcely had the order been given before one of the French ships raked the *Mars*. A cannon shot killed Duff and two seamen who were standing behind him. The ball struck the captain on the breast and carried off his head. His body fell on the gangway, where it was covered with a spare union jack until after the action.

Lieutenant William Hannah succeeded to the command of the *Mars*. The *Fougueux*, *Pluton* and other ships continued to fire upon the *Mars*, leaving her poop and quarterdeck almost clear of officers and men and her masts and rigging damaged so badly that she could not manoeuvre. She drifted north.

The *Tonnant*, 80, Captain Charles Tyler, was the fourth ship in the lee division. During the approach, she had changed places with the *Belleisle* in obedience to a signal from Collingwood made in view of the *Belleisle*'s superior sailing qualities. As the *Belleisle* passed, the two captains greeted each other, Tyler exclaiming, "A glorious day for old England! We shall have one apiece before night!"

The *Tonnant* steered for the gap between the *Monarca* and *Algésiras* and cut the line at approximately 12.20 pm. As she did so, she discharged her port broadside into the *Monarca* and her starboard broadside into the *Algésiras*. She then hauled up alongside the *Monarca*'s lee side, continuing at the same time to fire her starboard guns into the *Algésiras*. One of the *Tonnant*'s lieutenants subsequently described both enemy ships as being so close that a biscuit could have been thrown on board either of them. This position remained for some three-quarters of an hour, at the end of which the *Monarca* fell astern. It seems that she struck, but, with no British ship available to take possession of her, she rehoisted her colours. The *Monarca*'s withdrawal from the fray enabled the *Tonnant*'s port guns to fire into the *Pluton*, providing the *Mars* with timely relief.

The *Algésiras* attempted to cross the *Tonnant*'s stern and rake her. However, the *Tonnant* foiled this attempt and in doing so placed herself across the *Algésiras*'s bows, with the latter's bowsprit and anchors caught in the *Tonnnant*'s starboard main rigging. The Frenchmen attempted to board but were driven back by the forecastle guns loaded with grape and musketry from the marines. Only one

Frenchman reached the *Tonnant*'s quarterdeck, where he was pinned through the calf of his right leg with a half pike before a lieutenant stopped a second member of the crew from cutting him down and instead sent him down to the cockpit. Captain Tyler was shot through the thigh by a musket ball fired from the *Algésiras*'s rigging and was carried below, leaving Lieutenant John Bedford in command. Riflemen in the *Algésiras*'s tops inflicted many casualties. So close were the two ships that the *Tonnant* was firing lower deck guns without running them out. Both ships caught fire and the *Tonnant*'s firemen fought to extinguish it. Eventually the *Algéciras*'s three lower masts fell, having been shot through below deck. At about 2.15 pm, the second lieutenant with a boarding party boarded the Frenchman and carried her. Rear-Admiral Magon had been killed, 14 lower deck guns had been dismounted and the *Algéciras*'s port bow was a mass of splinters.

The *San Juan Nepomuceno* drifted close to the *Tonnant* and shot away her gaff. The *Tonnant* returned her fire and brought down her fore mast. The Spaniard struck soon thereafter, and the fourth lieutenant was sent with two men in the jolly boat to take possession of her. However, the boat was swamped on the way and the lieutenant, who could not swim, was saved by one of the men upon whom he later settled a generous legacy.

The *Tonnant*'s surgeon had instructed that tallow candles be held close to wounds so that he could inspect them; afterwards he discovered that his eyebrows had been singed away.

The *Bellerophon* was the fifth ship in the lee line. It had been Captain Cooke's intention to reserve his fire until passing through the enemy line but in view of the casualties and damage aloft, he decided to open fire about ten minutes before cutting the line, both to employ the men and also to cover the ship with smoke. She passed close under the stern of a Spanish seventy-four. So light was the wind that the *Bellerophon* was able to fire her carronades three times and every long gun on the port side at least twice. Her opponent's hanging magazine blew up.

The *Bellerophon*'s crew could see above the smoke the topgallant sails of another ship. This was the *Aigle*, a French seventy-four. The *Bellerophon* could not avoid running on board the Frenchman, with the former's starboard bow being on the latter's port quarter. The *Bellerophon*'s fore yard locked with the *Aigle*'s main yard. Cooke sent his first lieutenant, William Cumby, below to explain the situation to the officers on the main and lower decks. On his return along the main

'For Nelson Led Us On Our Way' by Harold Wyllie. View of the Battle of Trafalgar from the forecastle of the *Orion*. To port of the bowsprit, the *Conqueror* is firing at the *Bucentaure*. To starboard of the bowsprit, the *Victory*, *Redoutable* and *Téméraire* can be seen.

---

deck Cumby passed Overton, the master, who was being carried below with his leg shattered. Before he reached the quarterdeck ladder, Cumby was met by a quartermaster who had gone below to tell him that the captain had been shot.

Captain Cooke was mortally wounded at about 1.10 pm. Cumby had earlier in the day suggested to his captain that he should remove his epaulettes lest they should identify his seniority to enemy marksmen; Cooke replied that it was too late to do so. He was hit in his chest by a musket ball whilst reloading his pistols.

That morning, Captain Cooke and his first lieutenant had break-fasted together and at the end of the meal Cooke had shown Nelson's memorandum to Cumby. Upon perusing it, Cumby suggested that the master also should be apprised of it since whatever misfortune might strike captain or first lieutenant could well befall both of them and the master would be able to communicate its substance to whichever officer succeeded to the command. Cooke duly showed it to Overton. By now, the captain had been killed, the master mortally wounded and only Cumby remained.

The *Bellerophon* was still entangled with the *Aigle*. Although the *Monarca* on her port bow was nearly silenced, two other enemy ships on her port quarter were firing on the *Bellerophon*.

The *Aigle* proved to be a tough opponent. Two attempts were made by her crew to board the *Bellerophon*. During one of these, five Frenchmen had got onto the starboard spritsail yardarm and were making their way to the bowsprit when a seaman named McFarlane let go the spritsail brace so that the yard suddenly canted with their weight and they all fell into the water.

Musketry from troops on board the *Aigle* almost cleared the *Bellerophon*'s quarterdeck, poop and forecastle. Any possibility of boarding the Frenchman was out of the question in view of this hail of fire. Cumby ordered both those remaining on the poop and boarders who had been summoned to muster under the half deck ready to repel any attempt to board the *Bellerophon*. The *Aigle*'s men also threw

grenades on board the *Bellerophon*. One was picked up from the
gangway by Cumby whilst its fuse was burning and thrown overboard.
Another exploded, killing or wounding 25 men, one of whom in his
agony ran aft and threw himself out of one of the stern ports. These
grenades not only landed on the decks but were also thrown in through
the gun ports. One grenade, thrown through a lower deck port, blew
off the scuttle of the gunner's store room, set fire to the store room and
forced open the door into the magazine passage. Fortunately, the
doors were placed in such a manner that the same blast that opened
the store room door shut the door of the magazine. But for that, it is
probable that a fearful explosion would have destroyed both ships. As
it was, the gunner simply asked a lieutenant on the lower deck for some
hands to put out the fire, which was extinguished before more than a
few people realised what had happened.

At 1.40 pm, the *Aigle* hoisted her jib and dropped clear of the
Bellerophon, enduring a raking fire as she paid off. She was later
engaged by, and surrendered to, the *Defiance*. The *Bellerophon* took

possession of the *Monarca* at about 2 pm after a few shots. With no opponent nearby, the surgeon was allowed to perform some amputations in the captain's cabin.

The *Colossus* cut the line, discharged her opening broadside into the French *Swiftsure*'s quarter and then ran up alongside the *Swiftsure* to leeward. Having found employment for her port guns, the French *Argonaute* fell on board the *Colossus* to starboard. Their yardarms remained locked together for ten minutes or so, enabling the *Colossus* to inflict severe casualties upon the *Argonaute* before she broke loose. A few minutes later, the *Bahama* dropped astern and she and the *Colossus* fired at each other across the *Swiftsure*'s bows.

Welcome assistance arrived at approximately 2.30 pm in the shape of the *Orion*. Captain Codrington had worked her over towards Collingwood's ships, realising that they had greater need of reinforcement. Now she approached the *Swiftsure* as if to rake her. This induced the latter to make sail and, having done so, she soon found herself between the *Bahama* and *Colossus*. This at last enabled the *Colossus* to devote her entire attention to only one opponent. After firing several broadsides into the *Swiftsure*, the latter dropped astern and the *Colossus* laid into the *Bahama*. The *Bahama*'s main mast fell and soon afterwards she struck. The *Swiftsure* endeavoured to wear under the *Colossus*' stern, but the British ship wore quicker and discharged her starboard broadside, bringing down the *Swiftsure*'s mizen mast. The *Orion* then engaged the *Swiftsure*, whose main mast fell, and she surrendered to the *Colossus*.

At some stage, a cock escaped from the hen-coop on the *Colossus* and perched on the captain's shoulder, from whence it crowed loudly to the amusement of the men, who cheered.

The *Colossus*' casualty list of 40 killed and 160 wounded was the highest in the British fleet, although the *Victory*, *Royal Sovereign* and *Téméraire* all had more men killed. She had fought the *Bahama* for nearly, and the *Swiftsure* in excess of, two hours. In hauling up to take possession of her two prizes, the *Colossus*' mizen mast fell over the side.

The British *Achille* cut the line astern of the *Montañez* and engaged her from leeward for three-quarters of an hour or so, until the *Montañez* was driven out of the line to leeward. The *Achille* subsequently engaged the Spanish *Argonauta* from windward and eventually silenced her. The French *Berwick*, having already been in action, sailed between the *Achille* and the *Argonauta*. The *Achille* and

Berwick then fought each other, with the *Berwick* on the *Achille*'s starboard side; the *Berwick* struck to the *Achille* at 3.30 pm.

The *Revenge* fired upon the *San Ildefonso* before breaking the line astern of the latter ship and ahead of the French *Achille*. The *Achille*'s attempt to close the gap by making sail only just failed, although her bowsprit took the *Revenge*'s mizen topsail. The *Revenge* then hauled to the wind and engaged these two opponents from a position on the *Achille*'s lee bow. Later, the *Revenge* luffed up so that she could engage the *Achille* with her port guns and the *San Ildefonso* with her starboard guns. Subsequently, the *Principe de Asturias* joined them briefly and created a triangle around the *Revenge* before help arrived.

The *Defiance* attempted to cut the line astern of the *Principe de Asturias*, but the *Berwick* closed the gap and in doing so lost her bowsprit. Initially, the *Defiance* ran alongside the *San Juan Nepomuceno*, but realised that she had already surrendered to the *Dreadnought*. The *Defiance* engaged briefly the *Principe de Asturias*, whose opening shots carried away the British ensign. Seeing two other British ships coming up on the Spaniard's quarter, the *Defiance* pushed ahead and ran alongside the *Aigle*. Although already severely damaged, the *Aigle* offered stubborn resistance for a while before her fire slackened and Captain Durham, thinking that she had surrendered, decided to take possession of her.

An attempt to do so was made by a few men swimming over led by a master's mate named Spratt, who took his cutlass between his teeth as he swam across. He was able to enter the *Aigle*'s stern port, gained the deck, fought his way up to the poop and hauled down the French colours but was shot through the leg whilst doing so. He dragged himself to the ship's side and, holding his bleeding limb over the railing, called out to his captain before he swung himself back across to the *Defiance* by means of a rope. The other boarders also encountered resistance, so eventually they were recalled.

The *Defiance* hauled off. She and the *Aigle*, having rehoisted her colours, continued the engagement until the Frenchman struck at 3.30 pm. A lieutenant was sent over with a prize crew to take possession.

The remaining ships in Collingwood's division were the *Dreadnought, Thunderer, Defence, Swiftsure, Polyphemus* and *Prince*. Their lesser participation in the battle is reflected by their lighter casualties: in none of these ships did the number killed reach double figures. Not only did they have to overcome a light wind but also the fact that many

of the ships that they were pursuing had either bore away from the
original course or drifted to leeward. None had stories to recount that
compared with the leading ships although several performed valuable
service in the short time left before the end of the battle. Most of these
ships still found time to engage more than one enemy.

The *Dreadnought* engaged the *San Juan Nepomuceno*, which was
bearing down to rake the *Bellerophon*, silenced her after a quarter of an
hour, left her with only her main mast standing and sent a boat to take
possession. The *Thunderer* engaged the *San Ildefonso* and thereafter
the *Principe de Asturias*, which was Gravina's flagship. The *Swiftsure*
and *Polyphemus* both approached the *Belleisle* and drove away one
antagonist each. The *Prince* was a poor sailer and had been impeded
by having to shift a topsail. She engaged the *Achille* and then took
possession of the *Santissima Trinidad* some three hours after the
Spaniard had ceased firing.

The ships of Nelson's weather division entered the action well after
those of Collingwood's lee division. Nelson's leading ships were also
extensively damaged by the fire of the combined fleet as they sailed by
way of a feint towards its van.

The *Victory* was badly damaged during the approach. Most of her
casualties and damage suffered before she cut the line occurred after
12.40 pm, when she altered course by abandoning her feint towards the
van and steered instead to pass astern of the *Bucentaure*, which was
Villeneuve's flagship. The *Victory*'s mizen topmast was brought down
and her wheel was shot away, which resulted in her being steered by
emergency tackles rigged in the gunroom aft on the lower deck. One
shot killed Nelson's secretary.

The *Victory* cut the line at 12.45 pm and in doing so passed the
Bucentaure's stern so close that as she rolled her main yardarm
touched the rigging of the *Bucenature*'s gaff. The port 68-pounder
carronade on her forecastle had been loaded with one round shot and
a keg of 500 musket balls and it was now fired into the *Bucentaure*'s
stern with devastating effect. The other guns of the broadside, all either
double- or treble-shotted, were also discharged. Dust from the
Bucentaure's shattered woodwork covered officers on the *Victory*'s
quarterdeck.

The French *Neptune*, being to leeward, was able to rake the *Victory*
from ahead although she soon drew away lest the *Victory* might have
had any desire to run aboard her. Hardy now set the *Victory* alongside
the *Redoutable*. The *Victory* discharged her starboard broadside into

the Frenchman, with her boatswain firing the starboard 68-pounder carronade. The *Victory*'s starboard fore topmast studdingsail boom-iron caught in the leech of the *Redoutable*'s fore topsail. The *Victory* now concentrated upon the *Redoutable* to starboard, whilst firing her port guns at the *Bucentaure* and *Santissima Trinidad*. Hardy's decision to concentrate upon the *Redoutable* resulted in a gap opening astern of the *Bucentaure* for the following British ships.

A fierce action followed between Nelson's flagship and the *Redoutable*. The latter was to prove a formidable opponent. She was captained by Captain Jean Lucas, who had trained his crew to a high level of fighting efficiency by use of carbines, grenades, swords and pistols. His aim was to board his opponent, and earlier in the day his crew had exhorted him not to forget to board. Such was the emphasis upon boarding that, when preparing to do so, the *Redoutable* ceased firing; the silence of her guns twice induced the *Victory* to stop firing in the belief that the *Redoutable* had surrendered. Musketry and grenades from the *Redoutable*'s tops extracted a fearful toll on the *Victory*'s upper decks. The British did not share French enthusiasm for stationing musketeers in the rigging.

Nelson and Hardy had been pacing the quarterdeck sometime between about 1.15 and 1.35 pm, well after the two ships had come alongside each other, when just as they were turning near the ladderway, Nelson was struck in the left shoulder by a musket ball fired from the *Redoutable*'s mizen top and fell to the deck. In reply to his flag-captain's enquiry, Nelson replied, "They have done for me at last, Hardy." He was carried down to the cockpit by a sergeant major of marines and two seamen. As he was being carried below, he noticed that the tiller ropes needed attention and sent a midshipman to Hardy with a message to that effect. He then took his handkerchief from his pocket to cover his face in the hope that the crew would not identify him.

A few minutes later, the *Redoutable*'s crew attempted to board the *Victory*. Lucas, it seems, had noticed a slackening of the *Victory*'s fire - caused by the relative silence of the *Redoutable*'s cannon - and had received an unduly optimistic report as to casualties on the *Victory*'s unprotected decks. He ordered the *Redoutable*'s main yard to be lowered to serve as a bridge. A midshipman and four seamen reached the *Victory*'s decks by means of her anchor but were soon cut down. It was during this stage in the battle that Captain Adair, the *Victory*'s captain of marines, was killed by a musket ball in the back of his neck. One of his last orders had been to summon reinforcements from marines serving the guns below, and about 25 had answered the call. Although this order was inspired by the heavy casualties amongst the marines on deck, its timing enabled them to arrive just before the French attempt to board. Hardy also called for boarders, and seamen from the gun decks provided timely reinforcements.

The *Téméraire* had already been damaged before she joined the *Victory* and *Redoutable*. She also had suffered during the slow approach into battle and been raked from ahead by the *Neptune*. Just after the French attempt to board the *Victory*, the *Téméraire* fell on board the *Redoutable*'s starboard side with the Frenchman's bowsprit over her gangway somewhat forward of the main rigging and grappled her opponent. The *Téméraire* was therefore able to rake the *Redoutable* to destructive effect. Within a few minutes, the *Téméraire* had dropped alongside the French ship. The *Redoutable* was now between two British three-deckers, the *Victory* to port and the *Téméraire* to starboard.

The lieutenants on the *Victory*'s gun decks ordered the cannon to be loaded with three shot each and fired with a reduced charge of powder so as to avoid shot passing through the *Redoutable* and hitting the *Téméraire*. So close were the ships that the muzzles of the lower deck guns, when run out, came into contact with the *Redoutable*'s side. The fireman of each gun stood ready with a bucket of water, which was hurled at the shot holes in the *Redoutable* as soon as the gun had been discharged.

Amongst those who had been active on the *Victory*'s exposed decks was Midshipman Pollard. He had been exposed to dangerous fire from the tops: one bullet had damaged his telescope whilst he was holding it and another the watch in his fob pocket. He shot at and killed a number of Frenchmen stationed aloft, probably including the marksman who had shot Nelson.

Lucas decided at about 2 pm to surrender; the *Redoutable*'s colours came down with the fall of the mizen mast. Her contribution had been far beyond her size, since this mere two-decker had committed two British three-deckers to fighting her during the height of the battle. Her official casualty list was 490 killed and 81 wounded; Lucas' figures were 300 killed and 222 wounded. Hardy soon sent two midshipmen and some men over to the *Redoutable* to extinguish a fire. One of the two boats that the *Victory* had been towing astern was still usable, so they hauled in the painter, rowed over to the *Redoutable* and scrambled aboard through an open gun port. That they were favourably received was confirmation that the *Redoutable* had ceased hostilities.

The battered *Fougueux* drifted towards the *Téméraire* and received the British three-decker's starboard broadside, which had not previously been discharged, as she did so. She ran foul of the *Téméraire* at about 2 pm, so that four ships were then locked together. The *Téméraire*'s first lieutenant, Thomas Kennedy, led a boarding party to take the *Fougueux*. Amongst the master's mate, midshipman, 20 seamen and six marines with him was a seaman who had a union jack rolled round his neck. "It'll come in handy," he observed. It soon did, and within 10 minutes or so the *Fougueux* had been taken.

Five minutes or so later, the *Victory* broke away leaving the *Téméraire* sandwiched between the two Frenchmen. Hardy had been trying to free her, with the men using booms. The *Redoutable*'s main mast then fell across the *Téméraire*'s poop. Lieutenant John Wallace, the *Téméraire*'s second lieutenant, boarded and took possession of the *Redoutable* at 2.20 pm.

The *Neptune*, 98, Captain Thomas Fremantle, opened fire at 12.30 pm upon the *San Agustin* and soon thereafter on the *Héros* and *Santissima Trinidad*. Then she cut the line astern of the *Bucentaure*, discharging another raking broadside into the stern of the French flagship. After pouring several broadsides into the *Bucentaure* she passed on to engage the ship immediately ahead. This was the *Santissima Trinidad*, 130, the flagship of Rear-Admiral Cisneros, which had narrowly escaped capture at the Battle of Cape St Vincent. She was followed by the *Leviathan*, the fourth ship in the weather division, which also fired into the *Bucentaure*.

The *Conqueror*, 74, Captain Israel Pellew, raked the French flagship and then brought to on her lee quarter. After about a quarter of an hour of close action, the *Bucentaure*'s main and mizen masts fell over her starboard side, obstructing those of her guns that were still firing at the *Conqueror*. The fore mast followed some minutes later. The *Conqueror* had some assistance from the *Britannia* and *Agamemnon*, which both fired upon the *Bucentaure* from longer range. Villeneuve held hopes that he might be able to shift his flag to another ship, but all the *Bucentaure*'s boats had been destroyed.

The *Bucentaure* surrendered at about 1.45 pm. This was signified by the waving of handkerchiefs. Pellew sent his captain of marines, James

Atcherley, over in a boat with a corporal, two marines and two seamen. It seems that Pellew did not realise that his ship had been engaging the French flagship. When Atcherley boarded, he was met by Villeneuve and other officers.

"To whom have I the honour of surrendering?" Villeneuve asked in English.

"To Captain Pellew of the *Conqueror*," replied Atcherley.

"I am glad to have struck to Sir Edward Pellew," commented Villeneuve, mistaking Israel for his more famous brother, Sir Edward.

"It is his brother, sir," explained Atcherley.

"His brother!" exclaimed Villeneuve. "What! Are there two of them? Hélas!"

Atcherley considered that such senior officers should formally surrender to his captain. The *Conqueror* had drawn ahead to seek another opponent, so the Frenchmen were taken on board the *Mars* where they surrendered to Lieutenant Hannah.

Meanwhile, the *Neptune* had luffed up and brought to initially on the *Santissima Trinidad*'s starboard (lee) quarter, and later on her starboard bow. Her attack upon the huge Spanish ship was highly effective. The *Leviathan* thereafter brought to on the *Santissima Trinidad*'s lee quarter, and the *Conqueror* later positioned herself on the Spaniard's port quarter. The *Africa*, 64, had become detached from the fleet during the previous evening, having failed to see the signal to wear. She entered the battle by sailing along the line of the combined fleet to windward thereof, exchanging broadsides with ships as she passed them on the opposite course. She then closed with the *Santissima Trinidad* and positioned herself on the Spaniard's port (weather) bow.

The dismasted *Santissima Trinidad* was silenced by 2.15 pm and was rolling. Her officers decided to surrender by displaying a British flag at her lee gangway. The *Neptune* and *Conqueror* drew ahead to find other opponents. The *Africa* remained and Lieutenant John Smith was sent over to take possession of her. When he boarded, the Spaniards courteously informed him that they had not surrendered. There are two possible explanations. One is that the Spaniards considered it beneath their dignity to surrender to a mere sixty-four. The other was the approach of Dumanoir's ships from the north combined with the departure of the *Neptune* and *Conqueror*. The *Africa* would not have seen the flag displayed on the lee side. Whatever the reasons, and it may well have been a combination of these factors, it was not until about 5.30 pm that the *Prince* took possession of the *Santissima Trinidad*.

The van of the combined fleet played little part in the battle. Until steering towards the *Bucentaure*, the *Victory* had set a course aimed much nearer the van of the Franco-Spanish fleet. Not until relatively near did the *Victory* abandon the feint and steer towards Nelson's desired opponent. Neither Villeneuve nor Dumanoir, who commanded the van, took effective steps to rectify the situation. Villeneuve realised what was happening but, instead of making an unambiguous signal, merely hoisted at 12.30 pm an equivocal signal ordering those ships not engaged to take steps to get into action.

Dumanoir did nothing until it was too late. In his last signal, hoisted at about 1.30 pm or even later, Villeneuve ordered the van to wear and support the centre division. A combination of the light wind, the swell and incompetent seamanship resulted in further time being lost. Some ships had to lower a boat to turn around. The *Intrépide* ran foul of the *Mont Blanc*.

To counter the threat posed by Dumanoir's ships, at 2.30 pm Hardy signalled for ships to come to the wind on the port tack. Six ships, the *Leviathan*, *Conqueror*, *Britannia*, *Neptune*, *Ajax* and *Agamemnon*, and possibly also the *Africa*, responded and stood to the northward, to leeward of Dumanoir's flagship, the *Formidable*, and three other ships but to windward of other ships from the enemy van. Dumanoir had failed to keep his force together. The *San Agustin*, *Rayo*, *San Francisco de Asis* and *Héros* had wore and were appreciably to leeward of those ships that had tacked. The windward group exchanged broadsides with the British ships as they passed on opposite courses. The two ships at the rear of Nelson's line, the *Minotaur* and *Spartiate*, just managed to avoid being cut off from the main body of the fleet, crossing the bows of the *Formidable* and raking her in doing so. Ships that had been in the thick of the fighting, including the *Victory*, *Téméraire*, *Royal Sovereign*, *Mars*, *Tonnant* and *Bellerophon* also fired upon Dumanoir's line as it passed.

Dumanoir's four French ships, having passed to windward along the entire British line, then escaped to the south. Three ships from the Franco-Spanish van entered the main action and in due course surrendered. Other ships fled north-east.

The *Leviathan* engaged the *San Agustin* at about 3 pm. The *Leviathan*'s guns bore first and she discharged her port broadside, each cannon of which was treble-shotted, into the *San Agustin*'s starboard quarter and received only a feeble reply. To prevent the Spaniard wearing under her stern, the British ship ran on board the Spaniard with the latter's jib-boom caught in the *Leviathan*'s port main rigging. Further fire drove the Spaniards below and a boarding party led by the third lieutenant carried the *San Agustin* without further opposition at about 3.20 pm.

The *Africa* engaged the *Intrépide* by herself for at least three quarters of an hour. The *Orion* approached, fired upon the *Intrépide*'s starboard quarter, wore round her stern and brought to on the Frenchman's port bow and thus between her and the *Africa*. The *Intrépide* struck at 5 pm and was the last French ship to surrender.

The *Neptuno*'s captain decided after some indecision to join Dumanoir's four ships, but never succeeded because she was cut off and engaged by the *Minotaur* and *Spartiate*. She lost her mizen mast and both fore and main topmasts, and when she struck at 5.10 pm was the last Spanish ship to surrender.

Nelson's objective of creating a pell-mell battle had succeeded to such an extent that, as it progressed, the ships from the two original lines had become intermingled. Codrington wrote afterwards that, "We all scrambled into battle as soon as we could." Many ships on both sides must have engaged at least half a dozen enemy ships and the account given has concentrated upon the most prominent contests. A feature of the action had been the unusually high number of enemy ships boarded for a fleet action of the period.

Amongst the reasons for British success had been superior gunnery, ability to manoeuvre to good effect, and fighting in the confident expectation of victory. However courageous most of their adversaries had been, they were quite unable to match these qualities. These were factors that Nelson would have borne in mind when deciding upon his tactics.

Nelson had been carried down to the orlop deck, where he was tended by Dr Beatty, the *Victory*'s surgeon, and his assistants. Beatty examined Nelson and realised that the wound was mortal. The Rev Dr Scott and Burke, the purser, attended the admiral. Hardy came down twice, once at about 2.30 pm and again about an hour later; neither visit lasted for more than a few minutes. It was during the second visit that Nelson ordered the fleet to anchor and was kissed by Hardy. Some sounds of the battle could be heard, including cheers when enemy ships surrendered. When the *Victory* fired upon the ships of Dumanoir's squadron, Nelson remarked, "Oh *Victory*, *Victory*, how you distract my poor brain."

Nelson became steadily weaker. After saying and repeating several times, "Thank God, I have done my duty," he whispered, just loudly enough for Scott to hear, "God and my country." Nelson's death was recorded in the *Victory*'s log: "Partial firing continued until 4.30, when a Victory having been reported to the Right Hon. Lord Viscount Nelson, K.B. and Commander-in-Chief, he died of his wound."

At 4.30 pm, Gravina stood towards Cadiz and signalled for other ships to rally. His flagship was accompanied or followed by ten other ships.

One of the last events of the battle was amongst the most dramatic. The French *Achille* was by now the southernmost of the enemy ships. She had been engaged by several British ships before the *Prince* arrived. A few broadsides from the three-decker felled the *Achille*'s fore and main masts. Some ammunition in her fore top had already ignited and when the fore mast fell onto the boats, the latter were set alight and the fire spread. The *Achille* burnt for over an hour before she exploded well after 5 pm. Only about 140 were saved from her. Amongst the survivors was one Jeanette, who had stowed away on board the *Achille* to remain with her husband. During the battle she had assisted in distributing powder. She was picked up by a boat, taken on board the *Revenge* and reunited with her husband a few days later. Another survivor was a black pig, providing the midshipmen's berth of the *Euryalus* with pork chops instead of the usual fare.

British casualties amounted to 449 killed and 1,242 wounded. There were over 5,000 French and Spanish casualties. Amongst the latter was Gravina, who had been mortally wounded by the *Dreadnought*; he died four months later. Villeneuve was exchanged in April 1806, returned to France and was found stabbed to death.

A shot had entered a lower deck port of the *Revenge*, struck a gun and the fore mast before decapitating a young midshipman and killing seven men who were running out a cannon by severing them nearly in half, and finally embedding itself in the ship's side. On board the *Britannia*, one shot killed four and wounded six men. Another shot struck the muzzle of a gun on her lower deck, and split into fragments that killed or wounded everyone stationed there except for two persons. A double-headed bar shot killed eight marines drawn up on the *Victory*'s poop; this led Nelson to order the dispersal of the remaining marines and probably indirectly to his own death in that they were not in position to fire at the marksmen in the *Redoutable*'s mizen top. The captain's clerk of the *Victory* was killed by the wind of a shot passing close to his body without hitting him. Many casualties were caused by flying wooden splinters of up to several feet in length. Amongst the wounded lying below who joined in the cheering at an enemy ship's surrender was the *Royal Sovereign*'s master, who in consequence expired. Gangrene, tetanus, fever, disease and other complications resulted in the death of many wounded in the days after the battle.

The immediate tally after the battle counted the Franco-Spanish fleet as having lost 18 ships of the line. One, the *Achille*, had blown up. Seventeen ships were captured, of which eight were French and nine were Spanish. Unlike the Battle of the Nile, however, the victory did not provide Britain with several fine captured ships to take into service.

Nelson's death overshadowed the victory. Hardy had sent Lieutenant Hills in a boat with a message to tell Collingwood that Nelson was wounded but without saying that he was not expected to survive. Collingwood could read his expression, and both he and Blackwood, whose frigate had been summoned to assist the *Royal Sovereign*, realised the true state of affairs. When a parting shot from one of Dumanoir's ships cut the cable towing the flagship, Blackwood in the *Euryalus* sailed to the *Victory*. Once on her gangway, Blackwood was told that Nelson was still alive but he had died before Blackwood arrived in the cockpit. Word spread of their admiral's death and some crews guessed what had happened by the lack of lights that would usually have been visible from the stern of the *Victory*. Some ships, however, did not hear the news for several days. Many officers and men were reduced to tears. One officer wrote that they had lost the father of the fleet.

The British fleet did not heed Nelson's wish that it should anchor. He had issued a general signal at 11 am to prepare to anchor at the close of day, and the order he gave as he lay mortally wounded in the *Victory*'s cockpit for the fleet to anchor was relayed by Hardy to Collingwood. Initially, Collingwood dismissed the idea and ordered the fleet to sail west. By late evening, the swell had increased and he signalled "Prepare to anchor" but was dissuaded upon several ships reporting loss of anchors and severed cables. The *Defence* and three prizes did, however, anchor. Anchoring would have assisted damaged ships in urgent need of repair, helped to safeguard the prizes and allowed ships to provide mutual support to each other. A storm was likely, off a hostile lee shore with treacherous shoals.

Subsequent Events at Sea

The storm arrived on the morning of 22nd October. It lasted for a week, with a lull in the middle. Many found its experience far more terrifying than the battle itself. A few accounts of the many incidents of that week suffice to typify events that occurred.

The *Redoutable*, which had been towed by the *Swiftsure*, lost her last remaining mast during the afternoon of 22nd October. She made signals of distress and, despite the adverse conditions, boats from the *Swiftsure* picked up most of the prize crew and many prisoners. Later, Lieutenant Thomas Sykes, the *Swiftsure*'s second lieutenant, per-suaded his captain to allow him to attempt further rescue, and the launch rowed over. Because of the time taken and his increasing concern, the captain sent the pinnace under the command of the fourth lieutenant. The two boats continued to rescue Frenchmen until they were full. About 120 Frenchmen had been saved. The next morning, the *Swiftsure* saved 50 men on three rafts floating close to the ship.

The *Algéciras* was luckier. The prize crew from the *Tonnant* comprised 50 men responsible for about 600 captives. She had lost all three masts, her hull was battered with shot, and of her two remaining anchors, one had a broken shank and the stock of the other had almost been shot away. The prisoners were confined below, with gratings over the hatchways, but nobody could be spared from guarding them to rig temporary masts and sails. The prize crew anticipated that she might be wrecked and released her crew so that they might save themselves. The Frenchmen took their opportunity to recapture their ship and sailed her into Cadiz. The prize crew was returned to the fleet after being treated with the utmost kindness by the Spaniards.

On 23rd October, the *Fougueux* was wrecked; the remainder of her crew perished together with about 30 from the *Téméraire*. The *Bucentaure* was recaptured by her crew but was wrecked whilst trying to enter Cadiz. The same day, five Franco-Spanish ships of the line and some frigates attempted to retake some of the prizes. They secured the

Santa Ana, which Alava later claimed had never surrendered, and the *Neptuno*.

The *Naiad* had taken the dismasted *Belleisle* in tow but the stream cable parted during the evening of 23rd October. Because the *Belleisle* was dismasted, she rolled so deeply that water came in through ports and shot holes. Whilst trying to restore the tow, the *Belleisle* fell on board the *Naiad*, carrying away much of her starboard quarter and damaging her jolly boat. Squally weather led to the loss of the *Naiad*'s main topsail early during the following morning. At about 5 am, the *Belleisle* had drifted inshore so much that she was close to shoals east of Cape Trafalgar, with breakers only a mile to leeward. She managed to turn her head seaward and the *Naiad* stood towards her, sent a boat, took her in tow and hauled the *Belleisle* to safety. Both ships arrived safely at Gibraltar later the same day.

When the sloop sent by Blackwood to summon the ships that had been detached by Nelson entered Gibraltar Bay, the *Donegal*, 74, was alongside the mole. Her company made strenuous exertions to get ready for sea. She sailed out of the bay on 23rd October with her replacement fore yard towed in the water alongside her, not yet hoisted on board. Gradually, she clawed westward against a head wind, and the next day passed damaged British ships proceeding to Gibraltar and learnt of the battle and Nelson's death. Having joined the fleet on 24th October, she provided invaluable assistance to several damaged British ships and in rescuing men from prizes.

On 24th October at 8.30 am, Collingwood signalled to the fleet to prepare to quit and withdraw men from prizes after having destroyed or disabled them if time permitted. Later signals did mitigate this order somewhat. That same day, the *Indomptable* and *San Francisco de Asis* were wrecked whilst attempting to return to Cadiz. The *Rayo* rolled her masts over the side and was taken by the *Donegal*, but was later wrecked and the *Neptuno* also grounded.

Seven ships were lost on 26th October. The *Santissima Trinidad* and *Argonauta* were scuttled and sank, the *San Agustin* and *Intrépide* were burnt, the *Aigle* and *Berwick* were wrecked and the *Monarca* sank. Many wounded Frenchmen and Spaniards would have drowned below decks when these and other ships sank.

The barge's crew of the *Phoebe* frigate set fire to, and thus destroyed, the wrecks of the *Rayo* and *Neptuno*, both of which were aground west of San Lucar, on 31st October.

Amongst the detached ships was the *Canopus*, 80. When he heard the news a few days after the battle, Captain Francis Austen wrote of Nelson that, "he possessed in a superior degree the happy talent of making every class of persons pleased with their situation and eager to exert themselves in forwarding the public service."

The Spaniards displayed conspicuous kindness in the days after the battle. It was evident that they had a warmer regard for the British than for their French allies. A British master, who had been one of the prize crew of the *Rayo* when she was wrecked, arrived in Cadiz and was struck by the hospitality that he received. A carriage was backed into the water for him to step into from the boat, cordials and confectionery were placed in the carriage for him, women and priests presented him with delicacies as the carriage passed through the streets, and a bed and clean linen were prepared for him at a lodging. He commented later that he would have received nothing like the same amount of kindness had he been wrecked on the English coast.

Kindness was extended to French and Spanish prisoners. Captain Hallowell, who had missed the battle, sent Captain Infernet a trunk with shirts, stockings, some cloth to make a coat, a bed and a draft for £100 as acknowledgement of the treatment he had received when himself a prisoner. Codrington wrote to his wife asking her to provide Infernet with money.

A number of the British ships had been badly damaged. At Gibraltar, the *Belleisle* landed her most seriously wounded and was provided with jury rig: a main topmast served as main mast, fore topmast as fore mast, jib-boom as mizen mast and spare spars elsewhere. Many ships had sustained less but nonetheless significant damage: one shot-hole below the *Agamemnon*'s waterline was responsible for her taking in three feet of water per hour and necessitated much pumping. The *Conqueror*'s figurehead had been shot away and, at the request of her ship's company, on her return to England it was replaced with a figure of Nelson.

Rear-Admiral Dumanoir Le Pelley's squadron fled south on 21st October. A British frigate saw the French and lured them towards Captain Sir Richard Strachan's squadron, which began a chase. On 4th November, the French abandoned hopes of escape and prepared for action. In addition to his own ship, the *Caesar*, 80, Strachan had with him three seventy-fours, the *Hero*, *Courageux* and *Namur*, and two frigates. The French squadron, which had received some damage at Trafalgar, consisted of the *Formidable*, 80, *Duguay*

Trouin, 74, *Mont Blanc*, 74 and *Scipion*, 74. Cape Ortegal was the nearest land. The French ships surrendered within half an hour of each other. That they had resisted for as long as possible was confirmed by the fact that, within a short time of the end of the action, the fore masts of two ships were the only French masts still standing. French casualties totalled 730 as opposed to 135 British killed and wounded.

Dumanoir's failure at Trafalgar to support the centre of the combined fleet had become the subject of much criticism. This encouraged him whilst living on parole at Tiverton to write to *The Times*, which published his letter.

The ultimate fate of Villeneuve's fleet can now be summarised. One ship exploded on 21st October. Only four ships out of those captured during the battle remained in British possession to reach Gibraltar: the French *Swiftsure* and the Spanish *San Ildefonso*, *San Juan Nepomuceno* and *Bahama*. Dumanoir's four ships were captured on 4th November. Fourteen ships were destroyed during the week following Trafalgar, as recounted in the preceding paragraphs. Only ten survived in French or Spanish possession. Of these ten, eight (the *Principe de Asturias*, *Neptune*, *Héros*, *San Justo*, *San Leandro*, *Pluton*, *Montañez* and *Argonaute*) had fled to Cadiz and two (the *Santa Ana* and *Algéciras*) had been recaptured. It appears that only the *Neptune* and *Montañez* were fit for service.

Aftermath and Consequences

Collingwood despatched the *Pickle* schooner with his report of the battle. On 4th November she fell in with fishing vessels from Mousehole, which put in to Penzance with the news. The *Pickle*'s commanding officer, Lieutenant Lapenotiere, landed at Falmouth and travelled by post-chaise to London on a journey during which the horses were changed 19 times. He arrived at the Admiralty at 1 am on 6th November and announced to the First Secretary, "Sir, we have gained a great victory but we have lost Lord Nelson." A special edition of the *London Gazette* was published. The celebrations were muted because of Nelson's death. Robert Southey, the future poet laureate, wrote that, "Men started at the intelligence and turned pale, as if they had heard of the loss of a dear friend." A Day of Thanksgiving was held on 5th December.

Nelson's body was preserved in spirits and brought back to England in the *Victory*. An autopsy revealed that he had died due to the flooding of his lungs by blood. Upon his return, Nelson lay in state in the Painted Hall of Greenwich Hospital. His state funeral, which lasted for four hours, was at St Paul's Cathedral on 9th January 1806. Pasco was amongst the *Victory*'s officers who each carried a bannorel of lineage. Nelson was buried in a coffin that had been presented to him in 1799 by Captain Benjamin Hallowell, the *Swiftsure*'s captain at the Battle of the Nile the previous year. It had been made from the main mast of the *Orient*, the French flagship which had exploded during the battle; care had been taken to ensure that only material from the mast was used. The coffin was placed in a black marble sarcophagus in the crypt. Sir Isaac Heard, Garter King at Arms, having proclaimed Nelson's style and titles at the end of the funeral service, added thereto, "and the Hero who, in the moment of Victory, fell covered with immortal glory!"

Many rewards were bestowed following Trafalgar. Nelson's elder brother was awarded an earldom. Collingwood was created a baron. This caused him concern because he feared that he lacked the means to support the title and disappointment at refusal of his request that it be allowed to descend through a daughter, which he made because he had no son. Hardy received a baronetcy. Five of the first lieutenants were promoted to captain or, as it was generally termed, made post: the two whose captains had been absent, the two who succeeded to command during the battle after their captains had been killed and the *Victory*'s first lieutenant. Most of the other first lieutenants were promoted to commander on 24th December. Other officers also were promoted. The grade of admiral of the red was introduced in November as a mark of the navy's service during the year; the Admiralty announcement stated that the grade was being restored whereas it had never existed hitherto. The Patriotic Fund at Lloyd's, which had been launched in 1803, issued commemorative swords to the flag officers and captains, who also received medals. A Mr Boulton of Birmingham issued medals privately: gold ones for admirals, silver for captains and lieutenants and pewter for the others. Despite Nelson's wishes, the nation did not support Lady Hamilton, who died in poverty in 1815.

Prize money won was augmented by a special award of £300,000 voted by Parliament. Each captain received £3,362. Lieutenants, captains of marines and masters received £226 each. Civilian officers, standing officers and master's mates received £153 each. Midshipmen, gunner's mates and others in the same band won £37. Seamen each received £6 10s, of which £4/12/6d came from the Parliamentary vote and £1/17/6d as prize money. The special award was distributed in 1806 and the prize money in 1807.

Meanwhile, France won further military victories. The main French army, having marched from its encampments on the Channel coast, fought General Mack's Austrian army prior to its surrender at Ulm on 20th October 1805. Further Austrian forces surrendered before the end of the month. Napoleon had therefore defeated the Austrian army without having had to fight a major battle. The French then marched further east to fight the Russian army and found itself in increasingly inhospitable territory. Napoleon ensured that his enemies became aware of the plight of his army and thereby induced an attack. This resulted in the Battle of Austerlitz, fought on 2nd December, in which the French inflicted a crushing defeat on the Russo-Austrian army. The Treaty of Pressburg was signed on 26th December. These events resulted in the effective demise of the Third Coalition.

It is said that upon hearing of the Austrian disasters, Pitt, who was physically exhausted, pointed to a map of Europe and remarked, "Roll up that map; it will not be wanted these ten years." He died on 23rd January 1806 due to the effects of gout. Although he had been in some respects a poor military strategist by too readily allowing expeditions of negligible value, his determination to wage and win war had been unshakable in character and without equal throughout Europe. He is outstanding amongst British prime ministers for his overall record in both war and peace. His last speech had been on 9th November 1805, when at the Lord Mayor's banquet the latter proposed Pitt's health as 'The Saviour of Europe.' Pitt replied with only a couple of sentences. Having expressed his thanks and his view that Europe was not to be saved by any single man, he observed that, "England has saved herself by her exertions, and will, I trust, save Europe by her example."

Trafalgar proved to be a decisive strategic victory for several reasons. It is rightly regarded as being Britain's most emphatic naval victory. It removed the prospect of an invasion of Britain, although Napoleon did aspire in later years to invade Britain and by 1808 France had made significant progress towards rebuilding her battle fleet. The victory destroyed one of France's two main fleets and by doing so eased the burden on Britain's navy during its arduous roles throughout the following decade. The few enemy ships still in Cadiz surrendered in 1808 following the Spanish uprising against France.

Although the French fleet at Brest remained, it was easier to blockade this port than Toulon. Britain was assured a high degree of control over the Mediterranean although France did eventually build a new Toulon fleet. Collingwood succeeded Nelson as the commander-in-chief of the Mediterranean station; he remained abroad until illness caused him to set out to return to England in 1810 and he died soon after setting out on the passage home. Seldom did a French fleet venture to sea during the decade following Trafalgar. In the long term, Trafalgar led Napoleon to realise that his prospects of winning the war by invasion or other naval activity were so negligible that he would instead rely upon waging economic warfare; this led to France's eventual defeat.

Incidents, events and monuments have marked Trafalgar since the battle. In 1811 as Captain Hoste, who had served under Nelson, led his frigate squadron into action against a stronger Franco-Venetian squadron he signalled, "Remember Nelson." Annual celebrations held by Captain Cumby at Heighlington, his home village in County Durham, included a bonfire and events for the children, with the *Bellerophon*'s flag flying from the church tower. A monument in the form of an upturned telescope on Calton Hill in Edinburgh, overlooking the city centre from the north-east, was completed in 1815. The foundation stone of Nelson's Column in Trafalgar Square was laid in 1840 by the son of John Scott, Nelson's secretary who had been killed at Trafalgar.

The *Victory* remains the most significant relic of the navy of the era. The extent of her Trafalgar damage resulted in reduction of her armament and her being re-rated as a 98-gun second rate. Her most valuable service thereafter was in the Baltic. The *Victory*'s preservation is said to be due in part to Hardy, her captain at Trafalgar, cancelling an order that he had issued as First Sea Lord for her to be broken up, after expressing his regret to his wife. In 1922, she was taken from her moorings off Gosport to Number 2 Dock in Portsmouth Dockyard. In 1941, a bomb fell into the dock and exploded under the *Victory*'s port bow, creating a hole in her side but without inflicting mortal damage. She still serves today as the flagship of the Commander-in-Chief Naval Home Command and is open to the public.

RULE BRITANNIA

The navy's success is attributable to its consistent performance throughout the era. This chapter therefore examines a variety of actions, incidents and topics giving an overall picture of the navy.

Nymphe v *Cléopâtre* Frigate Duel

The first of many frigate duels of the era resulting in either side capturing the opposing ship was fought between the British *Nymphe* and French *Cléopâtre* on 18th June 1793.

The *Nymphe*, 36, Captain Edward Pellew, sailed from Falmouth on 17th June bound for Portsmouth. Pellew had experienced difficulty in completing his complement, but Cornish tin miners had augmented numbers and any opportunity to press from merchant ships had been taken. Shortly before sailing, Pellew heard that two French frigates had again been seen in the Channel.

The *Nymphe* sailed within sight of the coast until some miles west of Start Point on the south Devon coast, when Pellew ordered the officer of the watch to steer to the southward under easy sail by way of a speculative diversion to discover what they might encounter. At 3.30 am on 18th June a strange sail was sighted in the south-east quarter. The *Nymphe* bore up in chase under all sail. The stranger was the *Cléopâtre*, 36, Captain Jean Mullon, which did not answer the private signal but stood away from the *Nymphe*. The French frigate was probably only seeking additional time to prepare for action. At any rate, at 5 am she hauled up her fore sail and lowered her topgallant sails to await the British frigate.

At about 6 am, the ships were near enough to enable the *Cléopâtre* to hail the *Nymphe*. Pellew, not hearing exactly what had been said, merely replied "Hoa! Hoa!" This was immediately followed by his crew shouting "Long live King George" and giving three hearty cheers. Upon hearing this, Captain Mullon came to the gangway, waved his hat and exclaimed "Vive la nation!" by way of reply. Before or after this gesture, he addressed his crew briefly and waved a cap of liberty before them. The men shouted "Vive la republique!" in their turn. This cap of liberty was wooden, about seven inches long and painted red, with a round, tapering brass spear over three feet long with a screw at the end. It was given to a seaman, who ascended the main rigging and screwed it on the masthead.

Both ships mounted 12-pounders on their main decks. The *Nymphe*'s broadside was approximately an extra one seventh heavier than the *Cléopâtre*'s. The French ship had a larger crew, which had been together for longer than the British crew. Both captain and ship were probably amongst the best in the French navy. The seamanlike manner in which the *Cléopâtre* was handled did not escape Pellew's notice.

At 6.15 am, the *Nymphe* reached a position from which her foremost guns would bear on the starboard quarter of the *Cléopâtre*. Pellew's hat was still in his hand; this he now raised to his head as the prearranged signal to open fire. The antagonists continued to run before the wind, which blew from the port quarter, within hailing distance of each other. Both now and throughout the action the *Nymphe* was engaged on her port side only. After a spirited cannonade of a quarter of an hour, the *Cléopâtre* suddenly hauled up eight points from the wind as if wishing to turn away from the *Nymphe*. This was probably due to casualties amongst the men at her wheel.

Pellew's younger brother Israel, a commander, had recently joined the *Nymphe* as a volunteer. During the action, he took charge of the after guns and concentrated fire upon the *Cléopâtre*'s wheel. This fire killed the helmsmen and then shot away the wheel. It also brought down the mizen mast, leaving a stump about 12 feet above the deck. In addition to both misfortunes hampering manoeuvring, the wreckage from the mast obscured the fire of some of the *Cléopâtre*'s after guns.

This damage had been inflicted before 7 am, at about which time and as a result thereof the *Cléopâtre* paid round off, with her bow towards the *Nymphe*'s side. Soon afterwards, she fell on board the *Nymphe*, with her jib-boom passing between the British frigate's fore and main masts and pressing hard against the main mast. The *Nymphe*'s crew expected the mast to fall due to the damage it had already sustained and the fact that both the main and preventer stays had been shot away. However, the *Cléopâtre*'s jib-boom was carried away first, averting the threat to the *Nymphe*'s mast.

Pellew expected the Frenchmen to attempt to board the *Nymphe* and ordered the *Nymphe*'s boarders to be called to repel them. However, the *Cléopâtre*'s crew made no such attempt and Pellew issued orders for the *Cléopâtre* to be boarded. Lieutenant Amherst Morris, the first lieutenant, led a party over the *Cléopâtre*'s bows and Lieutenant George Luke, the second lieutenant, followed with another party. They fought their way along the gangways to the quarterdeck. The fury of the assault sufficed to result in the Frenchmen fleeing below or submitting, and her colours were hauled down by one of the *Nymphe*'s crew and British colours were hoisted. This literally signalled the end of the action, at 7.10 am. Pellew later wrote to his elder brother Samuel that, "We dished her up in 50 minutes."

Meanwhile, the frigates had fallen alongside each other. The *Cléopâtre*'s port bow was more or less opposite the *Nymphe*'s port quarter and the *Cléopâtre*'s port quarter likewise alongside the *Nymphe*'s port bow. The *Cléopâtre*'s port main topmast studdingsail boom-iron hooked the port leech rope of the *Nymphe*'s main topsail. This posed a new threat to the main mast. A maintopman named Burgess, spurred by Pellew's offer of a reward of ten guineas, climbed aloft and cut away the leech rope from the end of the main yard. In addition, Pellew ordered Lieutenant Richard Pellowe, the third lieutenant, to cut away the best bower anchor as a means of separating the ships. Despite these steps, it seems that the ships did not part until the last of the prisoners had been removed into the *Nymphe*.

Both ships had a casualty list amounting to approximately one fifth of their complement. The *Nymphe* entered the action with 240 men and boys and the *Cléopâtre* with a crew of 320. A perusal of these figures and the casualty lists indicate that the *Cléopâtre* finished the action with 67 effective men more than the *Nymphe*, which underlines the determination of the British boarders. The *Nymphe* had 23 killed and 27 wounded. These casualties were high for a victorious ship in a frigate duel and confirm that the *Cléopâtre* had been gallantly defended. The *Cléopâtre*'s total of killed and wounded was 63. Her captain, Mullon, had been mortally wounded by a round shot, which had torn open his back and carried away most of his left hip. Pellew attended Mullon's funeral and both wrote a letter of condolence and provided some financial assistance to his widow. The captured signal list was in due course delivered to the Admiralty.

The *Nymphe* had been extensively damaged aloft. Both fore and main masts had been badly damaged, the main sail had been shot to pieces, the lower rigging was badly damaged and the main, mizen and topmast stays shot away.

The *Nymphe* arrived at Portsmouth on 21st June with the *Cléopâtre*, and was cheered by the ships in harbour as she passed. News of the duel spread rapidly, resulting in rapturous celebrations and even the composition of a ballad. The king himself announced the news of the action from his box at the opera.

Captain Pellew was knighted at St James's on 29th June. His brother Israel was made post for his part in the action. The *Nymphe*'s first lieutenant, Amherst Morris, was made a commander and her master, John Thompson, was promoted to lieutenant.

Cutting-out of the *Hermione*

The cutting-out of the former *Hermione* frigate took place in 1799, two years after her company had mutinied in the Caribbean and taken her into a Spanish port. Her recapture was effected by the *Surprise*, 28, Captain Edward Hamilton. It was amongst the three most famous cutting-out actions of the era and was exceptional because it was almost unknown for such a large vessel to be cut out.

On 21st October, the *Surprise* arrived off Puerto Cabello on the Spanish Main and discovered the *Hermione* moored in the harbour with her sails bent and ready for sea. There were two strong batteries nearby.

After dinner on 24th October, Captain Hamilton gave details of his plans to the officers present. The hands were later sent aft, where he addressed them. Three tremendous cheers from his audience convinced Hamilton that his men were eager to take part. He added that he would lead the expedition in person, although doing so was habitually a lieutenant's role.

Those to take part were immediately mustered and preparations made. Every man was to be dressed in blue, with no white visible. 'Britannia' was issued as the password and 'Ireland' the answer. At 7.30 pm the boats were hoisted out.

The six boats were divided into two divisions, with the boats of each division to be in tow. The first division comprised the pinnace, the launch and the jolly boat, which were to board on the starboard (landward) gangway, bow and quarter. The captain, the gunner, a midshipman and 16 men were in the pinnace. The launch, under the command of a lieutenant, contained also a midshipman and 24 men. The jolly boat contained the carpenter, a midshipman and eight men. The second division consisted of the gig, black cutter and red cutter, which were instructed to board on the port (seaward) bow, gangway and quarter. They were commanded respectively by the surgeon, a lieutenant and the boatswain and each carried about 16 men.

The boarders were to take the first spell at the oars, with the boats' crews relieving them as they neared the *Hermione*. If the boats reached the *Hermione* undetected, only the boarders were to board, with the boats' crews remaining in their boats and taking the ship in tow as soon as the cables were cut. If they had been discovered, the boats' crews also were to board. Hook ropes were provided for towing. The *Hermione*'s quarterdeck was to be the rendezvous. The launch was to retain three men to cut the bower cable, for which purpose a platform had been erected over her quarter, and men in the jolly boat were to cut the stern cable. The gig was to send four men aloft to loose the fore topsail, the pinnace four men to loose the main topsail and the jolly boat two men to loose the mizen topsail.

As soon as the boats left the *Surprise*, Hamilton kept the *Hermione* in sight by standing up in the pinnace and using his night glass to steer a direct course for their quarry. When within a mile from the *Hermione*, the boats were discovered by two Spanish gunboats. The alarm was given, firing started and soon lights could be seen at the *Hermione*'s ports. The tow rope was cast off, Hamilton gave three cheers and ordered his men to row to the *Hermione*. His hope that the other boats would follow his example and ignore the gunboats was not fulfilled; some boats did engage them.

As the pinnace crossed the *Hermione*'s bows to take up her station, a shot fired from the forecastle passed over her. A rope, probably that of the anchor buoy, caught the pinnace's rudder, stopping her and causing the coxswain to report the boat as being aground. Hamilton realised that this was impossible, since the *Hermione* was afloat, and told the coxswain to unship the rudder. Since the pinnace's starboard oars were by now touching the *Hermione*'s hull, Hamilton gave orders to lay in the oars and board. The pinnace was then under the starboard cathead and fore chains. Hamilton slipped on some mud on the anchor, but retained his hold on the foremost lanyard of the fore shrouds, although his pistol was discharged accidentally during his struggles.

The pinnace's crew boarded at about midnight. Having cleared the forecastle, the boarders advanced to the break of the forecastle and saw the Spaniards on the main deck firing away, oblivious to the fact that they had already been boarded. They advanced along the starboard gangway towards the Spaniards on the quarterdeck, who came forward to engage them.

The gig's crew boarded on the port bow, moved along the port gangway to the deserted quarterdeck, but forgetting that the quarter-deck was the rendezvous then advanced along the starboard gangway. Although the Spaniards were now caught between two groups they managed to force the pinnace's men back to the forecastle. Hamilton was then left alone on the quarterdeck, where he was attacked by some Spaniards and badly wounded before some of his men returned just in time.

The black cutter had arrived. The first attempt by her men to board had been at the port gangway, her allotted station. As the men mounted the gangway steps, their lieutenant above them was knocked down, halting the advance, felling the men on the steps and injuring some of the men below. The cutter then pushed off and her crew attempted to board on the other side. When this failed, they returned to the port gangway and at last succeeded in boarding.

The marines were formed, a volley was fired down the after hatchway and the British charged down onto the main deck with bayonets fixed. About 60 Spaniards retreated to the captain's cabin and surrendered; they were secured and the doors closed. Fighting continued on the main deck.

The jolly boat arrived and her crew attended to its functions. Finally, the launch and red cutter arrived; they had been delayed by their irrelevant conflict with the guard boats.

Of equal importance to the fighting were the preparations to get the *Hermione* underway. The stern cable had been cut and the frigate was canting head to wind. The bower cable was now cut, the topsails were loose, the boats had the *Hermione* in tow and the gunner and two men (all three of whom had been severely wounded) were at the wheel and steered the ship.

The shore batteries opened fire upon the frigate. The main and spring stays were shot away, the gaff was brought down and several shot hit below the waterline. The Portuguese coxswain of the gig, who spoke Spanish, overheard plans to blow up the frigate. A discharge of musketry down the hatchway was sufficient deterrence, and by 1 am (nearly an hour after the pinnace had boarded) all opposition had ceased. At 2 am, by which time the *Hermione* was out of range from the batteries, the towing boats were called alongside.

The British loss amounted to only 12 wounded. Hamilton, who was knighted, suffered long-term effects from his injuries. The Spaniards had 119 killed and 97 wounded out of a crew of 365. The 231 prisoners were later put on board a schooner and landed at Puerto Cabello.

Cochrane and the *Speedy*

The 158-ton brig-sloop *Speedy*, 14, acquired a growing reputation in the Mediterranean from 1797 under three successive commanders, the last of whom was Lord Cochrane. Her exploits far outmatched her size since she was armed with mere 4-pounders as her main armament. Cochrane was a tall man and on one occasion he walked her deck with enough shot in his pocket for a broadside. The cramped nature of her commanding officer's accommodation was such that when he shaved he removed the skylight, stood up through its opening and used the quarterdeck as a table.

The *Speedy*'s exploits under Cochrane started on 10th May 1800 when she sailed from the south Sardinian port of Cagliari with a convoy of 14 merchantmen bound for Leghorn. Shortly after setting out, the *Intrépide*, a French privateer mounting 6 guns and carrying 48 men, captured a Danish brig in the convoy. Within three hours the *Speedy* retook the brig and captured the privateer. On 14th May, five armed boats set forth from Monte Cristo and took possession of the two sternmost merchantmen. A light breeze sprung up and Cochrane ordered the convoy to make its way to Longona. The *Speedy* took advantage of the freshening breeze and recaptured both vessels with their prize crews on board, although the boats escaped. On 21st May the convoy arrived safely at Leghorn.

Thereafter the *Speedy* formed part of the British squadron off Genoa, which was under siege by the Austrians, before leaving after the French surrendered. On 16th June the *Speedy* captured a tartan off Elba and sent it into Leghorn with a prize crew of an officer and four men. On 25th June she took a Spanish privateer anchored under a fort near Bastia on Corsica. Five gunboats thereupon left Bastia, chased

'HMS *Sophie* leaving Port Mahon', by Geoff Hunt RSMA.
The exploits of Cochrane and the *Speedy* formed the basis of *Master and Commander*, the first in the series of Patrick O'Brian's acclaimed Aubrey novels. The *Sophie*, which was the vessel in his book, was not an exact replica of the *Speedy*. Both were brig-rigged sloops.

---

the *Speedy* with her prize in tow and a running fight ensued until after midnight. The *Speedy* continued to be active during the following months. On 18th November she was nearly swamped in a gale, with the sea breaking over her quarter and considerable damage being inflicted. She therefore returned to Port Mahon, the navy's base on Minorca, and remained there until 12th December.

Such had been her depredations upon their coasting trade that the Spaniards sent ships to capture her. On 21st December 1800, an apparently well-laden merchantman was chased by the *Speedy*. Having decoyed the brig within hail, she raised her gun ports. Escape was clearly impracticable, but Cochrane had one stratagem available to him. He had heard at Port Mahon that the Spaniards were about to take exceptional measures to capture the *Speedy*. Cochrane therefore had her painted to resemble the Danish brig *Clomer*, which was well known on the Spanish coast. He even managed to obtain a Danish quartermaster and uniform for him. The *Speedy* hoisted Danish colours at her gaff and the Dane hailed the Spanish ship. The latter sent a boat to board the brig. The *Speedy*'s crew hoisted the yellow quarantine flag up to the fore. When the boat came within hail, the Dane informed its crew that the brig had left Algiers only two days previously and that the plague had been raging there. The pretence worked, and after exchanging greetings the brig and the boat parted company.

Duelling was fashionable amongst gentlemen of the period and a number of officers fought duels. Cochrane did so whilst in command of the *Speedy* during a brief visit to Malta in February 1801. Officers of a French royalist regiment held a fancy dress ball and Cochrane purchased a ticket. He chose to attend wearing a seaman's dress, complete with marlinspike and lump of grease as if he were working on the rigging. He was refused admittance upon entering the ballroom due to his dress and retorted by saying that he had not broken any rule. He was collared by a French officer, uproar broke out and he was taken to the guard-house. He was soon released, but the officer

demanded an apology and Cochrane refused. They fought a duel the next morning behind the ramparts. Cochrane's ball went through the Frenchman's thigh and the latter's shot passed through Cochrane's coat and shirt and bruised his side.

On 6th May 1801 at daylight off Barcelona the *Speedy* discovered a xebec standing towards her. Such vessels had prominent projections at both prow and stern, carried square and lateen sails according to the wind and were designed for Mediterranean conditions. She was the *Gamo*, 32. The complement of the *Speedy* had been reduced to 54 officers, men and boys because others were absent manning prizes, and she was armed with fourteen 4-pounders. The *Gamo*'s crew numbered 319. She mounted twenty-two 12-pounders on her main deck, and eight 8-pounders and two 24-pound carronades on her quarterdeck and forecastle. In both complement and weight of broadside, therefore, the *Gamo* had approximately six times the force of the *Speedy*. The Spaniard was equivalent in size to a small frigate.

Because of the light winds it was not until nearly 9 am that the two vessels were within gunshot. The xebec fired a gun and hoisted Spanish colours, to which the *Speedy* replied by hoisting American colours. To display false colours by way of deception was regarded as a legitimate tactic provided that true colours were hoisted prior to going into action. The brig later hoisted the British ensign whereupon the *Gamo* fired two broadsides without inflicting any damage. The *Speedy* reserved her fire for close range. She ran under the *Gamo*'s lee, her yards locked in the Spaniard's rigging and she discharged a double- or treble-shotted broadside. This first broadside apparently killed the Spanish captain, Don Fransisco de Torris, and her boatswain.

The British crew possessed one clear advantage during this opening stage of an apparently absurd duel. Such was the *Gamo*'s height out of the water that her shot merely passed over the *Speedy*'s hull. Although her rigging was badly damaged, she suffered few casualties. The *Speedy*, however, elevated her guns so that they tore into her antagonist's main deck.

The Spaniards endeavoured to redress the situation by boarding. Upon hearing the orders being given, the *Speedy* sheered off sufficiently to thwart the attempt and for good measure discharged a volley of musketry and a broadside before the Spaniards could recover. Two further attempts were made to board the *Speedy* but were thwarted.

Cochrane decided after the cannonade had lasted for at least three quarters of an hour that the time had come to board the *Gamo*. The *Speedy*'s surgeon, James Guthrie, took the helm and skilfully ran the *Speedy* alongside the *Gamo*. Cochrane then led his men onto their opponent. He had realised that boarding would be hazardous and ordered some of his crew to blacken their faces. These men boarded by the head, from which direction most of the Spanish crew were ready to repel boarders. The sight of diabolical figures emerging from the white smoke of the bow guns provided an unexpected dimension to the action and had the Spaniards at least momentarily transfixed. The *Speedy*'s men also boarded by the waist, where the conflict became particularly fierce.

For a few minutes, the outcome hung in the balance. Cochrane hailed Guthrie, who was still on board the *Speedy*, and ordered him to send another 50 men on board the *Gamo*. It may have been that there was nobody else left on board the brig, yet Guthrie indicated a readiness to comply that was understood by the Spaniards. The prospect of having been lured into a trap, with many men hitherto hidden below deck, weakened their enthusiasm for further resistance. Cochrane ordered one of his men to haul down the Spanish colours. The defenders assumed that their own officers had issued the order and all further resistance ceased some ten minutes or so after the *Speedy*'s crew had boarded.

British casualties had been remarkably light. The accounts do not tally, but the likely figures were three killed and five wounded during the cannonade and her lieutenant, the boatswain and one seaman wounded during the boarding. The *Gamo*'s casualties were 15 killed and 41 wounded.

Cochrane's problems were not yet over. He was fortunate in that the Barcelona gunboats did not attempt to rescue the *Gamo* despite having witnessed the action. Had they done so, the *Speedy*'s crew would have had difficulty in retaining their prize. The 263 unhurt prisoners were the main problem. They were driven into the hold, with guns loaded with canister pointing down the hatchways and men standing guard with matches lit. Cochrane's midshipman brother Archibald was prize master, with 20 of the *Speedy*'s crew on board the *Gamo*. Brig and xebec arrived at Port Mahon a few days later. The *Gamo* was not added to the navy, probably due to her rig, but was sold later to the Algerians.

The *Gamo*'s second-in-command, who had taken charge of the xebec after her captain had been killed, provided Cochrane with an unusual problem, which he solved with typical flair. He asked Cochrane to provide a certificate that he had done his duty. Cochrane duly gave him a certificate stating that he had "conducted himself like a true Spaniard", much to the latter's delight. Cochrane heard later that this document secured promotion for him.

In early June 1801 the *Speedy* fell in with the brig-sloop *Kangaroo*, 18. On 9th June, the two vessels attacked a Spanish convoy lying at anchor off Oropeso under a battery thought to mount 12 guns in a square tower. The escort consisted of a xebec mounting 20 guns and three gunboats. The British vessels anchored at noon and started to cannonade the enemy. The *Kangaroo* concentrated upon the tower and the *Speedy*, supported by a recently captured 6-gun privateer now used as a tender and commanded by Cochrane's brother, fired upon the escorts. After a while, a felucca mounting 12 guns and two more gunboats arrived. During the afternoon the xebec and at least three of the gunboats were sunk by gunfire. The tower was silenced by 7 pm although musketry from Spanish troops ashore continued until midnight. Of the ten merchantmen, three had been sunk and four had been beached, but boats brought out the other three, which were brigs laden with wine, rice and bread. The British vessels had almost no ammunition left.

The *Speedy* was ordered to escort a packet known to be a poor sailer to Gibraltar on the basis that the letter bag remained on board the *Speedy* until they were off the Rock, when it was handed over to the packet. Having fulfilled this bizarre arrangement, the *Speedy* ranged along the Spanish coast until she came across some anchored vessels which, upon the *Speedy* closing, were deliberately run ashore. Cochrane decided to set fire to them. One was laden with oil and the blaze that night attracted the attention of three French ships of the line.

All efforts to escape were in vain and the *Speedy* was captured on 3rd July. The captain to whom Cochrane surrendered declined to accept his sword in view of his heroic efforts to evade capture. Three days later as a British squadron approached, they sat down to breakfast but before it had ended a round shot crashed through the stern and shattered a wine bin. British success in the subsequent action ensured that a suitable enemy officer was soon available to be exchanged with Cochrane. He was made post with effect from 8th August, the day that the Admiralty received news of his acquittal for the *Speedy*'s loss. Bonaparte presented the *Speedy*, renamed *Le Saint Pierre*, to the Pope.

Amphibious Operations

The following narratives exemplify the range of the many such operations undertaken by the navy.

Curaçoa, the Dutch island in the West Indies, was sighted at 1 am on 1st January 1807 by the frigates *Arethusa*, *Latona*, *Anson* and *Fishguard* under Captain Charles Brisbane. Their plan was to take advantage of the fact that the Dutch defenders would have celebrated to excess on New Year's Eve. The attack was to be made on St Ann, on Curaçoa's south-east coast. Its narrow harbour, which contained a frigate and a corvette, was defended by forts.

The frigates entered the harbour at dawn. Although the *Fishguard* grounded, her three consorts anchored in good positions. With the *Arethusa*'s jib-boom over the town wall, Brisbane used her capstan as a table to write summoning the governor to surrender. He did not comply and action commenced. After a few broadsides, Brisbane led a boarding party onto the Dutch frigate whilst the *Anson*'s captain led his men onto the Dutch corvette; both were taken. They then landed with a force that stormed Fort Amsterdam, situated at the right of the entrance to the harbour. Having also taken the citadel and the town, the British force then returned to the ships and opened fire upon Fort Republique, which stood upon a high hill at the far end of the harbour. The island surrendered by noon. Surprise, speed and resolution had overcome a strongly defended position. The British squadron had lost only three killed and 14 wounded, and Brisbane was knighted.

On 13th March 1808, the *Emerald*, 36, whilst off the Spanish harbour of Vivero discovered therein a large French armed schooner, which proved to be the *Apropos*, and stood in to attempt her capture or destruction. She was faced by an outer fort to the right and an inner fort to the left. A landing party under Lieutenant Charles Bertram, the first lieutenant, drove the Spaniards from the outer fort. Meanwhile, the *Emerald* stood in as close as possible to the inner fort and opened fire. Another party under the third lieutenant was landed and engaged some soldiers, but could not find the inner fort. Soon most of the officers and men who had landed came upon the bulk of the *Apropos*'s crew. After an action involving musketry and the use of pike and bayonet, the French fled, leaving several of their number dead on the road. The British force approached the *Apropos*, which to avoid capture had run herself ashore at high tide. The *Emerald*'s party attempted, whilst under fire from soldiers, to get the schooner afloat but being unable to do so set her on fire and she exploded at 1 am. Bertram was promoted to commander due to this enterprise.

The activities of the *Imperieuse*, 38, Captain Lord Cochrane, from the summer of 1808 exploited the fact that Spain was now an ally of Britain.

In July, the *Imperieuse* was active along the Catalonian coast. Her crew blew up the strategically important coastal road and overhanging rocks and destroyed bridges to such effect that neither cavalry nor artillery could pass. Coastal batteries were destroyed and the guns at Canette were taken on board by means of hawsers slung between the cliff and the ship. On 31st July, the fort at Mongat, which commanded a pass on the road, was attacked by Spanish militia and the *Imperieuse*, which fired several broadsides at the fort before it surrendered. The captured French troops had to be protected from the Spaniards; they were taken off and the fort was blown up. Before the *Imperieuse* sailed the next morning, the British gave the Spaniards two of the field guns that had been captured together with powder and ammunition.

During late August and September, the *Imperieuse* cruised along the Languedoc coast of France. Signal stations were destroyed and signal books were removed. Coastal towns and ports were subjected to rocket attacks.

The *Imperieuse* and the *Spartan* frigate attacked the Isthmus of Leucate on 10th September. Boats disembarked landing parties, which took possession of batteries after enemy troops had fled, spiked the guns, blew up barracks and destroyed two vessels. As cavalry approached, the *Imperieuse* dropped anchor, swung round and at the moment that her starboard broadside could enfilade a gorge, Cochrane, from the masthead, directed a destructive fire of grape against the cavalry.

The *Imperieuse* arrived off Rosas on 20th November. The southern French army had been working its way to Barcelona and needed to take Rosas before progressing further. A party from the frigate took possession and held a decrepit fort next to the cliff edge until it was evident that negotiations for Rosas's citadel were in progress. That same day the British force climbed down rope ladders to the beach. Cochrane and the gunner were the last to leave and, as they did so, they fired trains leading to gunpowder, resulting in a massive explosion.

A French convoy with wheat bound for Barcelona for the supply of French troops was known to have entered the small port of Cadaques, north-east of Rosas. One morning at the end of December, before daylight, a kedge was dropped at the entrance to the port and the *Imperieuse* was warped in to the harbour. Both escorts, a cutter and a lugger, were fired upon by the *Imperieuse* and sunk by their own crews. Two parties of marines landed, one to make a feint near the town and the other between the town and the battery, whence the French were still firing. The troops stationed there presumably feared being cut off and ran to the hills. Five of the guns were subsequently taken on board the *Imperieuse* and the others were thrown over the cliff. The magazine was then blown up. Men in the frigate's boats thereafter boarded the merchantmen and took all 11 vessels. Snipers on the surrounding hills continued to impede operations until fire was directed at the rocks just behind them and showers of splintered rock silenced them. Over several days, the escorts were raised, careened, repaired and refitted; in due course they were taken out.

The *Anson* Shipwreck

The *Anson*, 38, Captain Charles Lydiard, sailed from Falmouth on 24th December 1807 to resume her station off Brest. A strong west-south-westerly wind delayed her arrival off the French coast until the morning of 28th December. As the gale was increasing, Lydiard decided to return to Falmouth and a course was set for the Lizard.

At noon, the sea was very high and the force thereof carried away three ports resulting in the *Anson* shipping a lot of water. The reckoning of her officers led them to believe that the Lizard was north by west some eight or ten miles distant. At 12.30 pm, land was seen which was probably Cudden Point but due to the thickness of the weather could not be identified. The *Anson* wore and stood south-east by east until about 3 pm, when the master suggested another attempt to make land and the frigate again stood in. The lead was cast and 27 fathoms sounded, which indicated that she was west of the Lizard. At about 4 pm, land was seen directly ahead and it was evident that the *Anson* was embayed.

The *Anson* was trapped in Mount's Bay to the west of the Lizard. She wore immediately and hauled to the wind on the port tack, but lost ground with every tack and about half an hour later those sails still set were furled. She anchored at 5 pm in 25 fathoms with the best bower anchor. The topgallant masts were lowered. The *Anson* rode at anchor until about 4 am on the 29th December, when the cable parted. The small bower anchor was let go and this held until it parted at 8 am.

Lydiard decided that he should concentrate henceforth upon saving life rather than his ship. There was no hope that a boat might come to their aid nor of even the strongest swimmer reaching the shore. He therefore ordered that the ship should be run as near to the shore as possible, the fore topsail was set and the master ran her onto the shingle forming the bar between Loe Pool and the sea, at the north-west corner of the Lizard Peninsular. The tide had been ebbing for nearly an hour when she grounded. The *Anson* broached to with her broadside heeling over and the deck facing the beach.

Some men were washed away by the sea sweeping over the deck and others were killed by falling spars. The crashing as they fell, roar of the sea, howl of the wind and shrieks of women on board increased the atmosphere of horror.

The main mast fell towards the shore. Lydiard, who was clinging to the wheel to avoid being washed overboard, encouraged his men to use it to try to reach the shore. Many did escape but some were washed off the mast. Most of those who left soon died whereas most of the survivors stayed until 11 am or so. The captain overheard the cries of a boy clinging to the wreckage, went over to him, and took hold of him by one arm whilst clinging to a mast with the other. Soon, a wave broke over them, the exhausted Lydiard lost his hold of the mast and they were both swept away.

Crowds of spectators lined the shore. Since the *Anson* had for some time been stationed at or near Falmouth, a number of relatives and friends of men aboard lived in the area. Several men tried to swim from the shore to the ship but were swept back exhausted onto the beach. Eventually, a powerful swimmer reached the *Anson*. The rope that he had taken with him was made fast to the wreck, and this lifeline enabled many survivors to escape. A Mr Foxwell, a Methodist preacher from Mullion, and Mr Tobias Roberts, a saddler from Helston, braved the surf and were followed by a few other people. They realised that some persons might still be on board but unable to help themselves. They discovered several persons lying below, all too exhausted to go up on deck. They saved some men and two women, but other men and two children were lost. Roberts kept guard over the stores and whilst doing so was attacked by plunderers, whose ringleader he seized and to whom he administered summary deterrence.

Most of the ship went to pieces at about 2 pm. By 3 pm, none of the *Anson*'s hull was still visible.

It is likely that about 60 of the ship's company, including her captain and first lieutenant, had died. The fact that many of the surviving men deserted increased the uncertainty as to the total number lost. Those men who remained were sent to Falmouth. Most of the bodies washed ashore were put into large pits without any burial rites, which was then customary. Ensuing indignation and the interest of Davies Giddy, a Member of Parliament for Bodmin, led to an 1808 act that required all bodies cast up by the sea to be interred in a churchyard or other burial ground.

The traditional court-martial to try the surviving officers and men was held on board the *Salvador del Mundo* at Plymouth on 6th January 1808. All were acquitted except for the master, who was admonished.

Henry Trengrouse, of Helston, had witnessed the wreck and been profoundly shocked. This caused him to design a life-saving rocket apparatus that fired a line from ship or shore and to which a hawser and chair were attached. Trengrouse's use of rocket instead of a mortar or other contemporary idea was that its gradual increase in velocity reduced the chance of line being broken; his apparatus was more portable and cheaper. It became, apart from the lifeboat, the most useful device in saving life following shipwreck. Trengrouse himself received negligible financial reward for his invention. Several of his rockets are in Helston's museum.

Escape from Valenciennes

Amongst the escapes from captivity in north-east France was that of four midshipmen from Valenciennes. They had been confined in the citadel and left on the evening of 16th November 1808. Boys and Hunter departed first, followed by Whitehurst and Mansell a quarter of an hour later. Conditions were ideal: it was blowing fresh, the sky was dark and cloudy and leaves were falling, rustling over the stones.

Boys and Hunter climbed a bank until they reached the parapet, and crept over and then down the breastwork towards the outer edge of the rampart. Boys forced first a poker and then a stake into the earth with his chest, slipped the eye of a rope over the head of the poker and fastened a small line from the poker to the stake. The rope was let down and they descended.

They crossed the lowered drawbridge, went along a passage and arrived at a locked door. Attempts to file the catch of the bolt, cut away the stone that received the bolt and use their picklocks all failed, so they decided to undermine the door. They were joined by Whitehurst and Mansell. Eventually they raised two pavement stones thereby creating a hole large enough to enable them to creep under the door.

The next obstacle was a raised drawbridge. There was, however, enough space between the top of the drawbridge and the arch above it through which they crept. They were now on top of the drawbridge and lowered themselves down by means of a second rope, which was passed round the chain of the bridge. They then landed on a handrail comprising two iron bars one above the other and remaining horizontal when the drawbridge was raised. Having kept hold of both parts of the rope in their hands whilst descending, the last man was able to bring it away. With their feet on the lower rail and their hands gripping the upper rail, the midshipmen crossed the gap. A second drawbridge was crossed in a similar manner.

They reached the upper citadel and made their way to the north-east curtain. Here they fastened the rope upon the breastwork and made their final descent, this time to freedom.

After the events of the last few hours, the midshipmen shook hands. They followed a footpath, with the north star serving as a guiding light. At one stage, a flash of lightning made them fear that the alarm gun had been fired and they ran for nearly half an hour. They passed through a small town and drank at the pump in the square. Later, four bandits rushed out from behind a hedge but were induced to keep their distance by a combination of threats and muttered conversation. The midshipmen had a brief sleep shortly before dawn, when they discovered and entered a nearby fortification.

Incessant rain delayed their departure until the late evening, when they ventured forth despite no improvement in the weather. They soon came to a turnip field, where they ate heartily. They passed through several villages during the night. Around dawn, they searched for a refuge and eventually saw a thicket surrounded by a wet ditch; they stayed in it until the evening.

The four entered a village, were later sheltered by a haystack and spent the following day hiding and sleeping in a wood. They left soon after darkness had fallen, walked to Deynse that evening and entered a public house. They learnt that conscripts were billeted about the town and gave the landlord to understand that they themselves were conscripts who due to lameness were allowed to travel at leisure. The landlord agreed and provided supper, after which they went to bed with each keeping watch in turn. The following morning, they bought spirits, paid the landlord and left.

At dawn on the Sunday, the group entered a wood and lay in the sun listening to church bells. Whitehurst had packed his prayer book, and they read prayers and offered thanksgivings. They entered Bruges towards midnight, wet to the skin, with bleeding and swollen feet, and entered a public house again pretending to be conscripts.

The journey continued towards Blankenberg, a coastal village a few miles east of Ostend. When four miles or so from the coast, they passed a solitary public house and saw four persons eating round a fire. Boys and Hunter entered with a view to purchasing provisions to take on board any vessel that they might be able to seize. Upon asking for gin, the landlady rose and stared at them before exclaiming, "Mon Dieu, ces sont des Anglais." She offered them all a meal and paid scant attention to their assertion that they were conscripts. She spoke of the happiness of her former service to an English family.

The four left, entered Blankenberg and ran down to the sea. Their exultation as they splashed about in it can easily be imagined.

They decided to return to the inn, which they entered at dawn. The landlady, Madame Derikre, readily offered further assistance and confirmed that she knew that they were British. Her public house was called the *Raie-de-chat*, which was usually abbreviated to Cat by her grateful guests. Situated midway between Bruges and Blankenberg, it was also a house of police correspondence and thus visited at least three times each week by gendarmes. A hayloft above the back room became the midshipmen's quarters. Its roof was open tiling through which the wind blew, so later on Madame Derikre suggested that they spend the nights below. She also put her guests in contact with persons who might be able to secure for them a passage to England, including a notary public in Bruges called Moitier.

The four escapees made many journeys to the beach at Blankenberg. On the last occasion they boarded a fishing schuyt, but when a local man gave the alarm they fled back to the Cat. Having left their knapsacks on the schuyt, they feared that the contents could lead their pursuers to the Cat.

Boys, Hunter and Whitehurst took all the bread in the house and set out for a wood on the far side of Bruges. Mansell, disguised as a girl, left to visit Moitier. The next three days must have been agonising. Mansell did not reappear, they did not know whether Madame Derikre was under suspicion or the inn under surveillance, they lacked shoes and their food had almost run out. They decided to return to the Cat. Whilst Hunter and Whitehurst remained under the hedge of the orchard, Boys approached the Cat and tapped at a window. Madame Derikre begged him not to enter and told him that, having escorted Mansell to Moitier, soon after her return gendarmes had conducted a thorough but fruitless search of the Cat. Boys left with bread, gin and cold potatoes and the three went to a wood.

When a peasant saw them two days later, they pretended to be conscripts but felt it wise to move to a thick wood about two miles east of the Cat. Colder weather set in and Whitehurst was ill for a period. Madame Derikre's son brought a horse cloth and she sent more food and gin. When snow fell, the three found a hollow from which a tree had been dug, laid a bed of dry twigs and formed a simple tent with the cloth propped up by a stick in the centre and fastened down by pegs with one corner left open.

In due course, they paid nightly visits to the Cat. They heard at last that Mansell had embarked for England in an open boat with a smuggler. Subsequently, Boys, disguised as a carpenter, went with Madame Derikre to Bruges to meet Moitier. Soon the three midshipmen were hidden away in a small house in a back street, with a poor friend of the owner lodging in the front rooms to alleviate suspicion and assist in the supply of provisions.

Moitier eventually brought news of a smuggler named Peter and his financial terms. The three comrades left Bruges later that evening with a guide, and walked towards Cadsand. They spent over a week in Peter's hut in the midst of the sandhills. At last, on 8th May 1809, definite information came to the effect that all would be ready at 10 pm. At that hour they walked down to the beach. A boat came silently towards the shore, with oars muffled. They embarked, each seized an oar and they rowed with all their strength.

The crossing to England was uneventful. The crew continued to row during the night. The boat had a sail, which a rising wind and sea induced them to close-reef at about noon. They fell in with a fishing smack at the back of the Goodwin Sands and were towed in to Ramsgate before landing at Dover at daylight on 10th May. Finally they took chaises for Betshanger, where Boys' father lived.

Civil Aspects

William Dillon was a 13-year-old midshipman on board the *Defence*, 74, at the Battle of the Glorious First of June, when he had charge of some guns on the lower deck. Social contact with captured French officers after the battle included a couple joining Dillon's party of midshipmen for a game of cricket, which in those days involved underarm bowling. Dillon was granted a few days' leave with his family, and returned to Portsmouth with his father. They dined at

Petersfield, where Dillon sought out Lieutenant Delille who was then living there on parole, and invited him to join them. Dillon's kindness towards the Frenchman led to his fellow travellers complimenting him for his consideration. Travel by land in those days was uncomfortable; the railway running south from Petersfield to Havant was not fully operational until 1859. Dillon and his father went on board some of the prizes in Portsmouth Harbour and dined later at the Star and Garter.

James Gardner was in 1797 a lieutenant in the *Hind*, then serving as a frigate attached to the Channel Fleet. The *Hind* captured the French privateer *La Favourite*, of eight guns and 60 men. Gardner was ordered to act as prize master, with two midshipmen and twelve men, and instructed to stay by the fleet. Once he had examined the prize, he recognised that she was in a bad condition. He therefore separated from the fleet and stood for the Channel.

In sailing up the Channel, *La Favourite* became caught in Portland Race. Gardner expected that the prize would founder. Being deep-waisted, he ordered her ports to be knocked out so as to allow the sea an unimpeded passage through. The hatches were battened down. The spray beat over the topsail yards and Gardner feared that they could have been washed overboard. They were able to haul off to the southward, to his immense relief. Most of the French crew had been removed following their capture; those who remained were terrified.

At daylight the following morning, they stood in to land and set course for Plymouth. Near Start Point, the prize crew hoisted a union jack over the French tricolour at the gaff. The jack blew away, and the halyards fouled so for a while they were unable to lower the French flag. A frigate therefore fired on them at long range but to no effect. The prize crew soon had the correct colours flying. That evening, they anchored in Cawsand Bay. Next morning, Gardner attended upon the port admiral, who agreed with his decision to leave the fleet and laughed heartily when told of the prisoners' panic.

Life on the lower deck was more congenial than has often been portrayed. Attractions included the prospect of prize money and definite employment. Life was made tolerable by alcohol, tobacco, singing, dancing on deck and women whilst in port. Grog, the usual strength of which was one part rum to three of water, was served twice daily. The need for men of war to carry a sufficient complement to man the guns ensured that there were plenty of hands to work the ship. Officers almost invariably treated them with a sound combination of fairness and firmness. Most men found the life acceptable and in some respects they were better off than they would have been ashore. Pay and leave were, however, major sources of discontent, and probably the main reasons for so many desertions. Wages during war were better on board merchantmen. Leave ashore was never guaranteed and at the end of a commission men were usually turned over, which meant being transferred to another ship without home leave.

An example of pressing occurred in the West Indies, when the *Crescent* frigate chased the *Trelawney* slaver and took 11 men. Other methods of compulsion included legislation passed in 1795, which applied to both counties and ports. Rye, for example, had to find 90 men. William Richardson had already served as a mate in the merchant service before being pressed. He was soon rated captain of the main top and was later promoted to quartermaster before acting as, passing the examination for and serving most of the era as gunner. The smuggler John Rattenbury was handed over to the navy, but he deserted only days later and returned home to Beer in Devon. Robert Hay and another man deserted from the *Ceres* guardship in the Thames; having procured bladders, shirts and straps for makeshift bags, they dived into the sea one night, swam ashore guided by a comet and eventually reached Maldon.

Flogging with a cat-of-nine-tails was the severest punishment that the captain could order. The ship's company assembled, the captain announced the punishment, the culprit was usually seized by his wrists and ankles to an upturned grating below the gangway or on the quarterdeck and the punishment was administered to the man's bare back by the boatswain's mates.

The day at sea was divided into watches, most of which were of four hours' duration. The bell on the forecastle announced time on the basis of one ring for each half hour after the start of a watch; thus three bells marked the time after one and a half hours. Most of the ship's company was divided into watches to take turn to be on duty; a two-watch system, with men spending half their time on duty, was usual. Calls were whistles used by the boatswain and his mates to pipe various orders, with their high pitch being audible above the noise of sea and weather.

Incidents added colour to naval life. The *Hind* frigate, which was sent to Norway, had a parrot which acquired the ability to imitate the boatswain's call so well that the men sometimes obeyed her orders. One day, some locals were invited on board in return for hospitality. A

Norwegian lady was being hoisted on board by means of a chair and whip on the main yard and had just been lifted out of the boat when the parrot piped, "Let go" and the men instantly obeyed, ducking the visitor in the sea.

Compasses were used for steering and to take bearings. Log lines run out astern from a reel held above a man's head with one end tied to a shaped piece of wood left floating was timed against a sand glass to measure a vessel's speed according to the number of knots tied in the line. Lead lines with a weight at the lower end of a line with a series of markings enabled the depth of the sea to be ascertained, which both checked whether there was a safe depth of water and also helped to locate the vessel's position. Sextants were hand-held instruments comprising a small telescope, mirrors and a calibrated brass arc used to measure angles between celestial bodies and the horizon; latitude was found by taking the noon sight of the sun and longitude by spherical trigonometry based on the moon and a star.

The *Investigator*, commanded by Matthew Flinders, sailed to the Pacific in 1801 to ascertain whether New Holland and New South Wales were separate or two parts of a larger continent. His detailed survey established that Australia, the name of which he suggested, was one continent.

An outstanding feat of seamanship saved the *Magnificent*, 74, from being wrecked near the Basque Roads on 17th December 1812 off a lee shore. During the previous night as conditions worsened, yards and topmasts were struck, the south-westerly wind increased, the ship rode at anchor and soundings with the lead located rocks. The gale and rain persisted, and the heavy sea could be seen breaking on the reef off the Isle of Rhe astern to the east. During the morning, the gale increased, the wind changed to west and a heavy sea pounded the port bow. It could only have been a matter of time before the hemp cables, which had been chafing on the rocks for hours, broke.

Preparations were made to save the *Magnificent*. The lower yards were swayed up to three-quarters their usual height, with the topsail yards on the caps. The courses and topsails were secured to their yards with yarn, ready to be cut in an instant. Some yards were braced up and others kept square. A hawser was passed through a port aft and bent to an anchor cable, ready to cant the ship to port. Captain Hayes addressed the ship's company, exhorted the men to carry out orders without hesitation and emphasised that, if they did not do so, they could not expect to survive. Meanwhile, the French were looking forward to gathering wreckage and were placing horses and carts along the shore.

The cables were cut, but when the hawser snapped, it was quickly cut with an axe. The helm was put hard over, the fore staysail hoisted, and the fore sail and fore topsail were both let fall and set so that they pressed against the mast. The ship now made sternway and turned in an arc with her head turning towards the reef. Once the wind was abaft the port beam, the mizen topsail was let fall and sheeted home, and the helm was shifted. Once the wind was right aft, the main topsail was let fall and sheeted home, followed by the main sail being set. Some yards were then braced up. This manoeuvre had been executed in minutes. The captain exclaimed, "The ship's saved", and soon thereafter the *Magnificent* anchored in the Basque Roads. In doing so, Hayes had used the weather to his advantage by taking his ship closer to the mainland to a safer position.

Napoleon's Surrender

The dramatic conclusion to the era was Napoleon's surrender. On 22nd June 1815, the emperor decided to abdicate and on 3rd July he left for Rochefort. The Admiralty suspected that Napoleon intended to escape to America and amongst the ships off the French coast under orders to keep watch for this possibility was the *Bellerophon*, 74. Her captain had received a note from a spy written on thin paper and placed in a quill warning him that Napoleon was heading for the coast. The former emperor embarked upon a French frigate, but it was evident that escape in anything other than perhaps a small vessel was out of the question so he decided to surrender.

On 15th July, following previous contact, the *Bellerophon* prepared to receive the former emperor. The waiting boatswain, Mr Manning, was approached by a midshipman who expressed a wish to have a relic of the occasion, grabbed part of Manning's whiskers and ran below as Manning threw his hat in his direction to the accompaniment of mirth. Napoleon boarded, surrendered to Captain Maitland and handed him a letter addressed to the Prince Regent seeking the protection of "the most powerful, the most constant and the most generous of my enemies." The *Bellerophon*, which was known to the men as *Billy Ruffian*, had fought in all three major battles of the era against French fleets. Napolean toured the ship and stated that he admired most the extreme silence and orderly conduct of the men. Somewhat later, he observed that, "Wherever there is water to float a ship, we are sure to find you in our way."

The *Bellerophon* returned to England with Napoleon and sailed to Torbay. Maitland received orders to prevent anybody except her crew from coming on board. The ship was surrounded by boats whose occupants desired to see the former emperor. Napoleon was often seen on deck by those in the boats, and upon sighting a well-dressed woman would take off his hat and bow. The *Bellerophon* sailed subsequently to Plymouth Sound. Here also many boats took sightseers, including Maitland's wife, to view the captive. The crew updated them by chalking messages such as "Gone to dinner" on boards and displaying them. Napoleon left a favourable impression with those whom he met. On 7th August, off Berry Head, Napoleon was transferred in a barge to the *Northumberland*, which sailed the same day to take him to the South Atlantic island of St Helena. He remained there until his death on 5th May 1821.

GLOSSARY

abaft   Closer to the stern than the location or object referred to.

block   A shaped piece of wood, usually holding one or more sheaves (q v).

careen   List a vessel to one side to expose her bottom for repairs or cleaning.

cutter   1 A single-masted vessel. 2 A type of ship's boat.

fathom   A measure of six feet, most used when referring to depth of water.

furl   Gather in and fasten a sail to its yard, stay or mast.

gaff   Spar rigged aft of mast and diagonally to extend upper edge of sail.

hawser   A small cable.

jury mast/rig   Temporary replacement mast/rig.

kedge   1 A small anchor. 2 Use thereof to warp (q v).

lateen sail   A triangular sail suspended from a diagonal yard.

lee   Facing away from the wind.

lee shore   Shore onto which wind blows, particularly if stormy.

luff   Alter course to sail closer to the direction of the wind.

lugger   A vessel with quadrilateral sails bent to a yard and set fore and aft.

marlinspike   Tool used for rigging.

ordinary, in   State of men of war laid up in reserve.

port   Left side of vessel etc (formerly larboard).

quarter   Ship's side towards the stern.

road	Place of anchorage on the coast at some distance from the shore.
schooner	Two-masted vessel with fore and aft sails suspended from gaffs.
sheave	Solid wheel with a groove around its outer circumference for a rope.
sheave hole	Narrow space in blocks, spars and elsewhere for sheave(s).
spritsail	Square sail spread from a yard below the bowsprit.
starboard	Right side of vessel etc.
tackle	Simple machine of block(s) and rope to enhance the rope's effect.
tartan	One-masted Mediterranean vessel, normally with a large lateen sail.
van	Foremost ship or division of a fleet or squadron.
warp	Move a vessel by pulling on a rope attached ashore, to an anchor etc.
weather	Facing towards the wind.

BIBLIOGRAPHY

Allen, Joseph, *Memoir of the Life and Services of Admiral Sir William Hargood*, 1841

Bennett, Geoffrey, *The Battle of Trafalgar*, 1977

Bourchier, Lady (ed.), *Memoir of the Life of Admiral Sir Edward Codrington*, 2 vols, 1873

Boys, Edward, *Narrative of a captivity, escape and adventures in France and Flanders during the war*, 1864

Chandler, David, *Dictionary of the Napoleonic Wars*, 1979

Clowes, W. Laird, *The Royal Navy*, vols 4 and 5, 1897–1903

Coad, Jonathan, *Historic Architecture of the Royal Navy*, 1983

Cumby, William, 'The Battle of Trafalgar', *The Nineteenth Century*, Vol XLVI (Nov 1899), pp 717–728

Dillon, William, *A Narrative of my Professional Adventures*, 2 vols, 1953–6

Dundonald, Earl of (Thomas Cochrane), *Autobiography of a Seaman*, 2 vols, 1860

Falconer, William (expanded by William Burney), *A New Universal Dictionary of the Marine*, 1815

Fenwick, Kenneth, *H.M.S. Victory*, 1959

Fraser, Edward, *The Sailors whom Nelson Led*, 1913

Gardner, James Anthony, *Above and Under Hatches*, 1955

Glascock, W.N., *Naval Officer's Manual*, 1848

Goodwin, Peter, *Nelson's Ships*, 2002

Grocott, Terence, *Shipwrecks of the Revolutionary and Napoleonic Eras*, 1997

Harland, John, *Seamanship in the Age of Sail*, 1987

Hay, Robert, *Landsman Hay*, 1953

Howarth, David, *Trafalgar: the Nelson Touch*, 1969

Hubback, J. H. and Edith C., *Jane Austen's Sailor Brothers*, 1906

James, William, *The Naval History of Great Britain*, 6 vols. The Chamier edition, 1837 has been used

Lavery, Brian, *Nelson's Navy*, 1989

Lever, Darcy, *The Young Sea Officer's Sheet Anchor*, 1808

Lewis, Michael, *A Social History of the Royal Navy*, 1793–1815, 1960

Lloyd, C. and Coulter, J. L. S., *Medicine and the Navy*, vol 3 1714–1815, 1957–1963

Lloyd, Peter, *The French are Coming!*, 1991

Lyon, David, *The Sailing Navy List*, 1993

Maitland, Frederick, *Narrative of The Surrender of Buonaparte*, 1826

Marcus, G.J., *The Age of Nelson*, 1971

Marshall, John, *Royal Naval Biography*, 4 vols and supplement, 1823–1830

Morriss, Roger, *The Royal Dockyards during the Revolutionary and Napoleonic Wars*, 1983

Murray, A., *Memoir of the Naval Life and Services of Admiral Sir Philip Durham*, 1846

Naval Chronicle, 1799–1818 (vol 19 covers the *Anson* shipwreck)

Nelson Society, *The Nelson Dispatch: Journal of the Nelson Society*, 1982 onwards

Nicolas, Sir Nicholas Harris, *The Dispatches and Letters of Vice-Admiral Lord Viscount Nelson*, 7 vols, 1844–46 (vol 7 covers Trafalgar)

Osler, Edward, *The Life of Admiral Viscount Exmouth*, 1854

Parkinson, C. Northcote, *Edward Pellew, Viscount Exmouth, Admiral of the Red*, 1934

Pocock, Tom, *Horatio Nelson*, 1987

Pope, Dudley, *The Black Ship*, 1963

Richardson, William, *A Mariner of England*, 1908

Senhouse, Humphrey, 'The Battle of Trafalgar', *Macmillan's Magazine* LXXXI, (April 1900) pp 415-425

Steel, David, *Elements of Mastmaking, Sailmaking and Rigging*, 1794 and later editions. Rearranged by Claude S. Gill for a 1932 edition

Sturges Jackson, Rear-Admiral T. (ed.), *Logs of the Great Sea Fights*, vol 2, 1900

Taylor, Rear-Admiral A.H., 'The Battle of Trafalgar', *Mariner's Mirror*, 1950, pp 281-321

Watson, J. Steven, *The Reign of George III*, 1960

Wyndham-Quin, W.H., *Sir Charles Tyler, G.C.B., Admiral of the White*, 1912

A total of approximately a hundred works, including the above,
have been consulted.

INDEX

NOTES ON COVER ILLUSTRATIONS

Front cover   'Nelson's Flagships at Anchor' (detail)
                      by Nicholas Pocock

Back cover   'Battle of Cape St Vincent' (detail)
                      by Sir William Allen

Both © National Maritime Museum, London

The front cover shows four ships closely associated with Nelson. To the right is the *Victory*, with stern galleries prior to her refit in 1803. Moving further left come three seventy-fours, the *Captain*, (Nelson's ship at the Battle of Cape St Vincent) showing port side forward, the *Vanguard*, (his flagship at the Battle of the Nile) with her port quarter and bow visible, and in front of her the *Elephant*, (his flagship at Copenhagen). These ships are painted as if anchored together at Spithead, off Portsmouth.

The back cover shows a starboard bow view of the *Captain* and further to the right of the picture two Spanish ships at the Battle of Cape St Vincent in 1797. Using his initiative, Nelson had left the line of battle. This painting captures the moment when he led a boarding party from the *Captain* onto the Spanish *San Nicolas*, 80, to port. Soon thereafter, they boarded the *San Josef*, 112, the stern and starboard quarter of which are visible towards the right of the picture.